North Dakota Legal Research

North Dakota Legal Research

Anne E. Mullins
Tammy R. Pettinato

Suzanne E. Rowe, Series Editor

CAROLINA ACADEMIC PRESS
Durham, North Carolina

Library of Congress Cataloging-in-Publication Data

Names: Mullins, Anne E., author. | Pettinato, Tammy R., author.
Title: North Dakota legal research / Anne Mullins and Tammy Pettinato.
Description: Durham, North Carolina : Carolina Academic Press, [2016] |
    Series: Legal research series | Includes bibliographical references and
    index.
Identifiers: LCCN 2016028055 | ISBN 9781611632002 (alk. paper)
Subjects: LCSH: Legal research--North Dakota.
Classification: LCC KFN8675 .M85 2016 | DDC 340.072/0784--dc23
LC record available at https://lccn.loc.gov/2016028055

Carolina Academic Press, LLC
700 Kent Street
Durham, North Carolina 27701
Telephone (919) 489-7486
Fax (919) 493-5668
www.cap-press.com

Printed in the United States of America
2019 Printing

For my parents, Bill and Kathy,
and
For Tim, Seamus, Belle, and Flick
—A.E.M.

For Alex, Eisen, and Layla
—T.R.P.

Summary of Contents

Contents

List of Tables and Figures

Tables

Figures

Series Note

The Legal Research Series published by Carolina Academic Press includes titles from states around the country as well as a separate text on federal legal research. The goal of each book is to provide law students, practitioners, paralegals, college students, laypeople, and librarians with the essential elements of legal research in each jurisdiction. Unlike more bibliographic texts, the Legal Research Series books seek to explain concisely both the sources of legal research and the process for conducting legal research effectively.

North Dakota Legal Research

Chapter 1

The Legal Research Process

I. Introduction

The key to effective legal research is knowing the research process and knowing how to adapt it to any situation. Sometimes you'll perform research in an area of law that you know well. Other times, you'll perform research in an area of law that is completely new to you. You need to know what the research process is and how to adapt it for these two different situations. In this book, you will learn the process of legal research, and you will learn how to adapt it to any situation.

II. Sources and Classes of Legal Authority

Legal authority is a source that tells you what the law is. As a legal researcher, you need to know the types of authority and how those authorities relate to each other.

A. Primary and Secondary Authority

All legal authority can be classified as primary or secondary. *Primary authority* is law, and it comes from a lawmaking government entity like a legislature, a court, or an administrative agency. Statutes, judicial opinions, and regulations are all examples of primary authority.

Secondary authority is not law. Instead, secondary authority tells us what the law is or how the law applies. Secondary authority might come from legal experts in a particular field, like practicing lawyers, professors, and legal editors. Practice guides, treatises, hornbooks, legal encyclopedias, and law review articles are all examples of secondary authorities.

B. Mandatory and Persuasive Authority

Mandatory authority is the term used to describe law that a court must apply to a dispute before it. The law of a particular jurisdiction is mandatory within that jurisdiction. Mandatory authority is also called *binding authority* because it is the law that binds the court and the parties within the jurisdiction. In dealing with a dispute that is governed by state law in North Dakota, the mandatory authority — i.e., the law that a court deciding the dispute must apply — is North Dakota state law. In a dispute that is governed by federal law in North Dakota, the mandatory authority is federal law from the Eighth Circuit and the U.S. Supreme Court.

Persuasive authority is not binding, but a court may choose to apply it or to rely on it for guidance. Primary authority from another jurisdiction is persuasive authority. In addition, all secondary authority — i.e., authority that is created by non-lawmaking entities, like practitioners, professors, and legal editors — is persuasive authority. In a dispute that is governed by state law in North Dakota, persuasive authority would include federal law and law from other states. In a dispute that is governed by federal law in North Dakota, persuasive authority would include federal law from circuits other than the Eighth Circuit (because the Eighth Circuit is binding in North Dakota) and law from all states.

Novice legal researchers often ask how persuasive different types of persuasive authorities are. The answer varies. With respect to primary authorities, the higher the level of court that the authority comes from, the more persuasive it generally is. There is usually no official difference between opinions that come from the same level of court. For example, in North Dakota, the First Circuit Court of Appeals is officially just as persuasive as the Ninth Circuit Court of Appeals. And one trial court is equally persuasive as another. But, there are certain judges who are extremely well respected and whose opinions might therefore be particularly persuasive. Similarly, there are jurisdictions that have expertise in certain substantive areas of law, and their opinions in that area might be particularly persuasive. For example, the Eastern District of Texas has been handling a high volume of patent infringement cases for many years. As a result, an opinion from that particular jurisdiction on patent law might be more persuasive than an opinion on patent law from a district court that does not handle many patent infringement cases. When you don't have the inside scoop on what court or judge might be especially persuasive, you should determine the persuasiveness of an authority based on how relevant it is to the issue you're researching and how well reasoned it is.

C. Hierarchy of Authority

Although all mandatory authority is binding, that authority is not created equally. There is a hierarchy of mandatory authority. Within each jurisdiction, the relevant constitution is the top authority. Everything must comply with the constitution. Statutes come next, and regulations follow statutes. Next in the hierarchy is case law. When an issue isn't controlled by statutory law or regulatory authority, it is controlled by common law—i.e., judge-made law. The next section explains that lawyers usually research statutes and regulations before researching cases. That's in part because statutes and regulations are higher in the hierarchy of authority than cases, so it makes sense to research them first.

III. The Legal Research Process

This section describes the different steps in the research process. These steps are also summarized in Figure 1-1. As discussed further below, the order in which you take these steps will differ depending on the information with which you start your research and your level of familiarity with the issue.

Figure 1-1. The Research Process

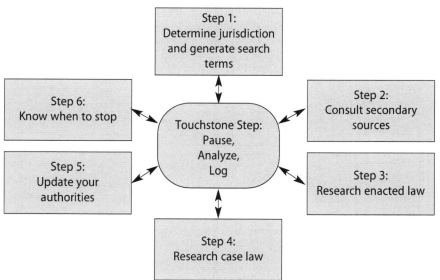

A. Step 1: Gather the Facts, Determine Your Jurisdiction, and Generate Search Terms

The first thing to do when you undertake a research project is to gather facts about the issue you're researching. You gather facts by talking to the client and senior lawyers and by reviewing documents relevant to the project. Chapter 3, Receiving Research Assignments and Gathering Facts, discusses fact gathering in further depth.

Once you have gathered the facts, you need to determine which jurisdiction's law controls: it could be state, federal, tribal, or local/municipal law. It's important to know which law controls because that tells you which authority is mandatory and which authority is persuasive.

Once you have determined which jurisdiction's law controls, you need to generate terms to guide your research. These are your *search terms*. When you begin a research project, you may know a great deal about the area of law you're researching, or you may know absolutely nothing at all. Regardless of how much you know, take a moment and think about what search terms might be useful to you in conducting your research. Generating search terms is important when you already know the area well because having a set of terms to review as you conduct your research will keep you from pigeonholing yourself. Generating search terms is important when you don't know the area of law you're researching because it gives you a starting point in your research.

To generate search terms, brainstorm a list of words that are relevant to your topic. Sometimes, the key term or terms are fairly obvious. If you have a client who has been arrested for disorderly conduct, then "disorderly conduct" is probably going to be your best search term. Even so, you should think of other ways that a court or legislature might say "disorderly conduct." "Breach of the peace" might be another way that a court or legislature might say disorderly conduct, so you'd want to add that to your list of terms. Sometimes the key terms aren't so obvious, and you'll have to listen closely to your supervisor or your client to identify possible terms. Some lawyers find that asking themselves the questions a journalist reporting on the issue would ask can yield good starting search terms. Who? What? When? Where? Why? How?

After you get a starting list of search terms and you start working with them, you'll probably discover that some of your initial search terms don't work well, and you'll discover new terms through your research that work very well. That doesn't mean that your initial list of terms was a bad one; in fact, the opposite is true. Research is a process, and some leads will pan out and others won't. As a result, the research process isn't linear—in other words, you don't just move through it hitting each step once and progressing to the next step. Instead, you come back to repeat different steps in the process as you learn more and more about an issue. Although generating search terms is certainly one of the first things you'll do when you undertake a research project, it's not something you'll do only once. Instead, the more you learn about your particular issue, the better developed your list of search terms will become.

B. Step 2: Consult Secondary Sources

Secondary sources are the resources that make up secondary authority, discussed above. Secondary sources explain the law. Sometimes they offer analysis, sometimes they compile primary law, sometimes they do both. Secondary sources include materials like legal encyclopedias, treatises, hornbooks, and law review articles. When you don't know much about the issue you're researching, secondary sources are an efficient and low-cost way to get background information on your issue. They will help you refine your search terms, and they will sometimes even give you citations to relevant primary authorities.

Secondary sources are absolutely crucial to the success of efficient researchers of all levels, from novice to veteran. While you can get good information on an area of law from a judicial opinion, remember that a judicial opinion is tailored to a particular narrow issue. So, what might look like extensive background in an opinion is typically only a piece of the picture. Secondary sources, however, will usually give you the big picture. As a result, they frequently help you identify important considerations that you might not be experienced enough to spot. You need to be able to set yourself up to identify those issues. Secondary sources are key to helping you do that.

This book covers secondary sources in Chapter 4.

C. Step 3: Research Enacted Law

Once you have some background information on the issue you're researching, you'll want to check to see if there are constitutional provisions, statutes, or regulations that apply to your issue. Typically, the most useful enacted law resources to use are *annotated*. Annotated resources include not only the text of the law, but also lists of cases and other sources that analyze the law.

This book covers constitutions in Chapter 5, statutes in Chapter 6, legislative history in Chapter 7, and regulations in Chapter 8.

D. Step 4: Research Case Law

By the time you turn to researching judicial opinions, you will frequently already have some citations to cases that you can look up immediately. You will have gotten these citations from secondary sources, annotated enacted law resources like annotated statutory codes and regulatory codes, and even from senior lawyers on your team. Continuing case law research apart from those steps is important to ensure that your research is thorough.

Even if you don't have any case citations, you'll be able to find judicial opinions using three primary techniques. The first technique is searching in a *digest*. When opinions are published, legal publishers like Thomson Reuters Westlaw and LexisNexis review the cases to identify the different areas of law that the opinion covers. The publishers then put cases that cover the same areas in print compilations or online databases that researchers can access. The second technique is *topic searching*. In addition to digests, online databases also group cases into topical groups or outlines. You can find what you're looking for by browsing those topical groups or outlines. The third technique is *word searching*. You can use online databases to search for specific words and phrases in judicial opinions.

This book covers case law research in Chapter 11.

E. Step 5: Update Your Authorities

The law is not static. Laws and legal principles change, get withdrawn or overruled, and spark commentary in other sources. Therefore, you need to know whether the authorities you're using are still good law, and you also need to know what kind of commentary those authorities have sparked. You can do this by *updating*. When you update, you'll not only learn whether the law is still good law, but also you'll discover other sources that have cited to the law that you're updating. Therefore, updating also functions as a powerful research tool.

This book covers updating in Chapter 12.

F. Step 6: Know When to Stop

The most difficult part of the research process is knowing when to stop. Generally, you can stop when two things have happened: First, you have read (and re-read) your authorities and you are confident that you have filled all gaps in your analysis; second, you start seeing the same authorities again and again as you work through the research process. Having an effective and well documented research strategy will help you stop when it's time to stop.

IV. Executing a Research Strategy

When you are practicing law, you need to get the right answer to every client every time, and you need to do so efficiently. Knowing how to execute a research strategy is key to establishing yourself as a successful researcher.

A. The Process Takes Many Different Paths

The strategy that you execute will depend on the issue you're researching, how complex the issue is, and your level of familiarity with the issue. Once you've determined your jurisdiction and generated research terms, your next step could be any number of things. The steps laid out in Figure 1-1 are numbered, and if you know nothing about an issue, you will probably follow them in roughly that order (though you will repeat some of the steps multiple times). But depending on what information you start with, you might not follow them in numerical order. Here are just a couple of possible paths, with the numbers inserted to show the steps in Figure 1-1:

- If you know nothing about an issue, you'll start by consulting secondary sources (2). From there, you might find a citation to a statute that controls the issue (3). From there, you might look the statute up in the annotated code and get a handful of case citations (4). You can use those cases to find other cases and statutes. When you update (5), you might find even more cases. You might then shore up your research by checking the case digests (4).

- If your supervisor has given you a citation to a key case when she gives you a research project, then it's best to start by looking up that case (4). From there, you might find citations to a relevant statute (3) and other cases both within the text of the opinion and when you update the case (5). When you look up the statute in the annotated code, you'll find more citations to relevant cases (4). When you look up the cases from your initial opinion and from the annotated code, you'll find more sources, perhaps a secondary source that explains how various jurisdictions address the issue (2). You might then shore up your research by checking the digests (4). When you check the digests, you might find a related issue that you realize you need to research as well, so you might then check further statutes in the annotated code (3), etc.

As you can imagine after reading the above two scenarios, the strategy you follow will adapt to the issue you're researching. Moreover, while you will exercise some control over your strategy, the steps you take will necessarily be determined in part by what you find along the way. So, how do you execute a research strategy in light of those conditions? You remain aware of the steps of the process, you analyze your results, and you log your work. This is the touchstone of the research process, and you will perform it repeatedly throughout the research process.

B. The Touchstone: Pause, Analyze, and Log

First, you must ensure that you remain aware of each step in the process and consider whether you need to conduct that step. Throughout this book, you will learn that there are some steps that you should probably hit every time you research an issue. There are some steps that you might be able to skip because of the type of issue you're researching or your level of familiarity with the area of law. But, you always need to make intentional and thoughtful decisions on which steps to take and how to take them.

Part of making intentional and thoughtful decisions requires being aware of the decisions that you have already made. This awareness is more important than ever when you're using online research sources (which you will be using primarily, if not exclusively). It is incredibly easy to click-click-click your way into a research vortex, where your sense of time disappears and, along with it, your sense of what you're looking for and what you've accomplished. *Pausing* as you work through each step of the process and reflecting on your progress will help you keep focused and aware of your work. *Analyzing* the sources that you find along the way will deepen your knowledge base as you work through the process. A deeper knowledge base will enable you to refine your search terms and to make savvy choices about which steps to take next. Finally, creating a *research log* will give you a record of the steps that you have taken throughout the process. As a result, a research log is a powerful tool that reminds you where you've been and helps you decide where you're going.

To create a research log, follow these steps:
- **Write what you know.** Briefly describe what you know about the issue.
- **Boil it down.** Then, take that general description and boil it down to a single sentence issue statement that describes what you're researching.
- **List your initial terms.** Create an initial list of search terms.
- **Make a map.** Quickly map out which steps you expect to follow and which sources you expect to use along the way.
- **Take notes.** As you look up your search terms in each source, take notes on what search terms you use in which source. Then, take notes on what you discover in each source. If a source has no helpful information,

make a note of that, too. Taking notes on your work will keep you focused on your process. It will also save you from inadvertently re-tracing your steps down the line.

- **Refine your search terms.** As you learn more about an issue, your list of search terms will become more refined. Make a note of any new search terms as you move through the process, and determine whether you want to go back to a source you've already searched with your new terms.

- **Analyze and reflect.** As you work through your research process, periodically analyze what you have found so that you deepen your understanding of your issue as you work through the research process. Reflect on which sources you need to revisit to fill analytical gaps.

- **Keep your log!** You'll want to keep your log after you have finished your research project for two key reasons. First, your log will help you answer questions about your research. Senior lawyers will frequently ask you questions about your research, and they will sometimes do this several weeks after you've completed a project. Keep your log and consult it when you're answering questions. Second, your log will help you undertake related research projects. Having a past log on hand to refresh your memory will jump start your research process on related projects.

Keeping a research log will feel time consuming at first, but the more proficient you become at research, the easier logging your work will become. And, as an added bonus, your research logs can help refresh your memory about the research process in general when you find yourself tasked with a research project in an unfamiliar area of law.

Chapter 2

Research Techniques

I. Introduction

Chapter 1 introduced the research process. This chapter focuses on research techniques that will help you as you work through that process. The following chapters will delve more deeply into the various sources that you will use when researching.

II. The Basics

A. Capitalize on the Work of Others

Experienced legal researchers start with the same ace up their sleeves: They know to capitalize on the work of others. When you begin a research project, ask yourself whether there are materials available that can give you a jump start on the research process. The most common materials are secondary sources. Covered more specifically in Chapter 4, secondary sources are commentary that explains the law and provides cites to primary authority.

In addition to secondary sources, you can take advantage of your own past work or the work of others in your law office. Past memoranda, motions, and briefs can be helpful starting points. If you're not sure whether there is helpful past work in your office, ask a colleague whether the office has handled cases in that area before. Additionally, most law offices now have online document management systems. These systems typically have word searching capability, so you can plug in some of your search terms and see what comes up. You might just find recent work on the same issue that provides a sense of the area of law and some citations to start your research. You might even be able to use parts of the documents to paste into your own, giving you a jump start on not only your research, but also your writing.

B. Vet Your Resources

Research projects can be overwhelming, especially when you're on a tight timeline. It can be tempting to just dive in and start researching at full speed. But taking a moment to thoughtfully vet your resources will help you use your precious time much more efficiently.

Before selecting and using any resource, ask yourself the following questions:

1. Is it relevant?

- What jurisdiction does the resource cover? Is that the jurisdiction that you need?
- What type or types of authorities does the resource contain? For example, if you're looking for statutes, does the resource include statutes, or does it only include regulations?

While authorities from other jurisdictions or other types of authorities can sometimes be helpful in advancing your research, the most efficient way to start is within your own jurisdiction and with the type of authority you need. If you do not find sufficient material within those parameters, then you can expand to other jurisdictions and other types of authorities.

2. Is it current?

Whether your source is current is a three-part question.

- First, does the source you're using include authorities from relevant time periods? For example, some online databases cover only certain date ranges or stop coverage after a certain date. You must be aware of what time periods the database you're using covers. Many online databases include a "scope note" that provides information about the content of the database, including the covered time periods. Some scope notes also contain useful tips about searching in the database. In Lexis and Westlaw, the scope note is a button with a lowercase "i." Other databases might have the word "scope" or "contents" or something similar.
- Second, if you're using print resources, is there any updated information affecting your source? Updates are often provided in a *pocket part*, which is a supplement that is periodically added to the inside of the back cover of a print volume to provide relevant information that came out after the volume was printed. Some print resources instead provide supplemental pamphlets that are shelved next to the volumes they update.
- Third, are your resources still valid law? As noted in Chapter 1, you can determine whether your resources are still valid law through a

process called updating. The process allows you to see how subsequent authorities have treated the resources you plan to rely on, for example noting that a case was reversed on appeal or a statute has been amended. Updating is covered in detail in Chapter 12.

3. Should I use print or online resources?

To choose the most effective and efficient medium, ask yourself these questions.

- Where is the document I need available? Almost all recent primary authority is available online; some secondary authorities are likewise available online. Significantly, however, some older primary authority and many secondary authorities are available only in print.

- Are online documents official? Sometimes it can be fairly easy to find a source online. But, what you find might not be the official version, and, as a result, it could materially differ from the official version. This does not mean that online research should be viewed with suspicion. It simply means that you need to be thoughtful about how you use online searching. Frequently, a quick online search can reveal an unofficial version of a source that you need. You can then use information that comes with the unofficial version to quickly track down the official version in another medium, either the official online version or the official print version.

- What is the easiest way to search the source? Sometimes, you'll be looking for a very specific word or phrase, and online searching—either through search functionalities or even the find function on your keyboard—will be easiest. Other times, you'll benefit from flipping through pages of a book to get a broad overview of a statutory scheme, for example, or an area of law in a secondary source. You might want to flip back and forth from the table of contents to the index as you search. Other times, you'll want fast access to additional authorities, and online hyperlinks will be very useful. As you become familiar with different sources, think about ways that you can search each. Over time, you will likely develop preferences for which medium to use to search a particular source. Experienced researchers frequently report that they prefer to research statutes and secondary sources in print, and cases online.

- What is the most economical way to find what you need? Your clients won't have to pay for print resources, but your clients will have to pay for your time. Print research can be time consuming. Online services can be lightning fast, but access to them can be very expensive. How to choose? Much will depend on the type of contract you have with on-line services. Contracts vary widely: Your office might pay a monthly fee that then gets divvied up and billed to clients for their proportion of use. Your office might pay by amount of time spent on the service. Your office might pay by the search, with the price determined by the database used. Or your office might have some other arrangement entirely. The first step to determining whether print or online is most economical is to find out how your office pays for online research. In a large law office, an office librarian will be able to share these details with you. In a smaller office, ask an administrative assistant for guidance. If you decide to research online, you will then need to decide the most efficient and cost effective way to conduct your research there. Once you have made these two determinations, you can adjust your research strategy to ensure that you are spending your time and your client's money wisely.

III. Online Resources

A. The Major Commercial Resources

Lexis and Westlaw are the predominant online legal research resources. Both offer collections of up-to-date primary authorities, like cases and statutes, and extensive collections of secondary sources, like treatises and law reviews. Both also include news sources, practice tools (e.g., forms), and public records information. Because of the vast amount of available information, searching in Lexis and Westlaw can be costly.

B. Other Commercial Resources

Other commercial providers, such as Fastcase and Casemaker, are available to the legal community. Many of these providers are less expensive than Lexis and Westlaw. Notably, Casemaker is free to members of the North Dakota bar. If you have limited resources, as many small offices and solo practitioners do, you should consider whether Casemaker or one of the less expensive alternatives can meet your needs. The skills you develop using one online platform are easily transferable to other online platforms.

In addition to general online resources, there are specialized databases that some researchers find helpful or even necessary to their practices. For example, Bloomberg BNA and Commerce Clearing House provide online databases for subjects such as tax, health law, and business and finance. HeinOnline provides law journal articles and some other legal authority. Be sure to ask your law office librarian or check your law office's law library page to determine whether you have access to any specialized databases. And, as noted below, you can access HeinOnline through the University of North Dakota Thormodsgard Law Library website.

C. Free Online Legal Resources

Finally, some online legal resources are free. The websites of governmental bodies and educational institutions are the most common. The website for the North Dakota legislature has links to the state constitution, the Century Code, session laws, and administrative rules.[1] The Thormodsgard Law Library website offers access to a variety of resources, including the law library catalog, HeinOnline, LegalTrac (a legal periodicals index), and the Foreign Law Guide (codes and other basic legislation from foreign jurisdictions).[2] Two useful sites outside of North Dakota are the Library of Congress's Guide to Law Online[3] and Cornell University's Legal Information Institute.[4]

In addition to governmental and educational websites, other free sites are beginning to offer legal resources. Google Scholar offers cases and law journal articles.[5] You can access these items through Google Scholar's "Legal opinions and journals" option. Another place to access legal scholarship is the Legal Scholarship Network on Social Science Research Network (SSRN).[6] Finally, even Wikipedia can function as a quick secondary source for legal terms and doctrines, major cases, and major legislation. As with any source that is not professionally provided, you must always verify what you have found.

IV. Online Searching

There are many different ways to search online resources. Sometimes you will check an index and link to the relevant material, sometimes you will browse a table of contents and link to relevant material from there, and sometimes you will perform a full-blown database search. Some database search techniques are intuitive; others are more of a learned skill. This section reviews the two

---

1. The address is www.legis.nd.gov.
2. The address is law.und.edu/library.
3. The address is www.loc.gov/law/help.
4. The address is www.law.cornell.edu.
5. The address is http://scholar.google.com.
6. The address is www.ssrn.com/lsn.

most common database search techniques, natural language and terms and connectors.

A. Natural Language Searching

Lexis, Westlaw, and some other databases offer natural language searching. This is essentially Google-esque searching in which you select the database you would like to search and then enter a short query or key terms. The service searches the entire database of documents for your terms and returns results in order of relevance. See Figure 2-1 for an example of a natural language search on Lexis.

Figure 2-1. Natural Language Search on Lexis

Type in your query, make sure you have selected North Dakota as your database filter, and click the search button.

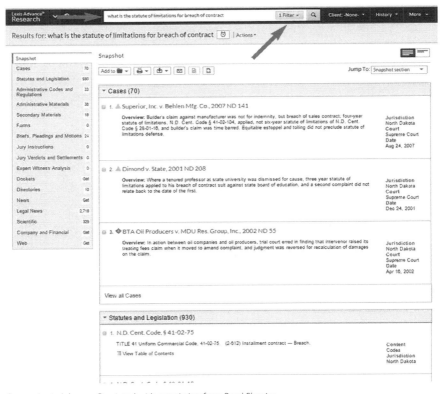

Source: Lexis Advance. Reprinted with permission from Reed Elsevier.

Each database uses its own algorithm to find and rank search results. One of the things that Lexis and Westlaw appear to search for are results with high concentrations of your search terms. But it is not clear exactly how each service conducts its searches. To underscore that point, note that the same search in Figure 2-1 would produce results in a slightly different order if conducted on Westlaw.

Although the search algorithms are not transparent, the search capability using natural language has improved markedly in recent years, especially on Lexis and Westlaw. As a result, while most researchers once used natural language searching as a way to follow up after terms and connectors searching, many researchers now start with natural language searching and follow up with terms and connectors. Regardless of how effective natural language searching currently is, keep in mind that you do not know exactly how the search engine is pulling results. Thus, an important source might not appear, or it might be so far down the list of relevant results that you might overlook it. Try to always follow up your natural language search with some well crafted terms and connectors searches.

B. Terms and Connectors Searching

Where natural language searching is broad and Google-esque, terms and connectors searching is specific and technically precise. "Terms" refers to your search terms. "Connectors" refers to the words or symbols you use to connect those terms in a way that tells the database how you want it to search for your terms in relation to each other. For example, you might want to see all documents that have the word "breach" appear within two words of the word "contract." Terms and connectors searching lets you do that, and much more. You can look for words within the same sentence or paragraph, you can look for specific phrases, and you can even exclude certain words from your search.

As you can probably see, both the greatest benefit and greatest drawback of terms and connectors searching is the highly precise nature of it: It allows you to find exactly what you're looking for. But you also risk inadvertently excluding relevant results with an under-inclusive search. Before natural language searching was as effective as it currently is, terms and connectors was the default language search. Now that natural language searching is so effective, it seems to have become the default. Regardless of which you start with, however, it's a good idea to shore up your research by running the other type of search to ensure that you have collected all relevant results.

To conduct a terms and connectors search, first determine which databases you want to search. If you want to search everything (cases, statutes,

Figure 2-2. Narrowing Your Databases on Westlaw

Select the appropriate tab and go from there.

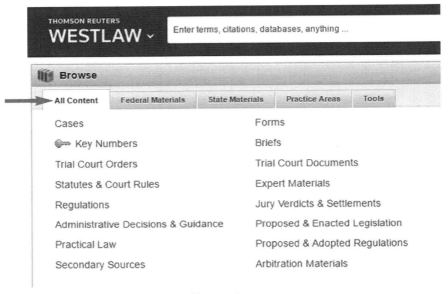

regulations, secondary sources, etc.) in a particular jurisdiction, simply select the jurisdiction in the search box at the top of the Lexis or Westlaw home page. But, before you do that, you should know that providers like Lexis and Westlaw will charge more money for you to search broader databases. Therefore, it makes sense to narrow the database if you can. For example, if you're looking for case law from North Dakota, it makes sense to limit your search to North Dakota cases. You can limit your databases on Lexis by clicking "filter," and then selecting the appropriate categories from there. Similarly, on Westlaw, you can limit your databases by selecting the appropriate tab on the Westlaw home page and moving from there. See Figure 2-2.

After you have selected your database, you then craft a search using terms and connectors in the search box. See Table 2-1 for a chart of the most common terms and connectors on Lexis and Westlaw.

You can add parentheses to give priority to certain connectors. Doing this functions much like a math problem. Assume you want to conduct a search to find documents containing either physician or surgeon, within the same

Table 2-1. Most Common Terms and Connectors

Goal	Symbol	Example
To find documents with the exact terms inside the quotation marks	" " to find exact terms leave a blank space between each word to find the terms plus variations (like plurals and possessives) (Lexis)	"search and seizure" (Lexis and Westlaw) search and seizure (Lexis)
To find documents that contain both terms	& AND	dog & bite; dog AND bite
To find documents that contain either or both terms	or (Lexis and Westlaw) a space (Westlaw)	physician or surgeon (Lexis and Westlaw) physician surgeon (Westlaw)
To find documents in which the terms appear in the same paragraph	/p	fraud /p ponzi
To find documents in which the terms appear in the same paragraph, with the first search term appearing before the second	+p	slip +p fall
To find documents in which the terms appear in the same sentence	/s	emotional /s distress
To find documents in which the terms appear in the same sentence, with the first search term appearing before the second	+s	reckless +s intent
To find documents in which the search terms appear within n number of words of each other	/n	efforts /4 secrecy

Table 2-1. Most Common Terms and Connectors, *continued*

To find documents in which the first search term precedes the second term by *n* words	+n	violent +3 tumultuous
To find documents that do not contain the term	and not (Lexis) but not (Westlaw) % (Westlaw)	homicide and not negligent (Lexis) homicide but not negligent (Westlaw) homicide % negligent (Westlaw)
To find words with different endings	!	possess! = possessor, possession, possessing, possessed
To find words with anything where the universal character symbol appears	*	Feinb*rg = Feinberg, Feinburg
To find documents before or after a certain date or within a certain date range	To search before a date: Date(<xxxx) (Lexis) Da(bef xxxx) (Westlaw) To search after a date: Date(>xxxx) (Lexis) Da(aft xxxx) (Westlaw)	Before 1995: Date(<1995) (Lexis) Da(bef 1995) (Westlaw) After 1995: Date(>1995) (Lexis) Da(aft 1995) (Westlaw)

sentence as medical malpractice, and in the same document as knee. Your search would look like this:

(physician or surgeon) /s medical malpractice & knee (Lexis)
(physician surgeon) /s "medical malpractice" & knee (Westlaw)

You can limit your search to certain parts of documents. On Lexis, these are called *segments*; on Westlaw, they are *fields*. For example, to search for an opinion by Judge Bye, you would include the segment or field that provided the judge's name:

Judge(Bye) (Lexis)
ju(Bye) (Westlaw)

Figure 2-3. Lexis Advanced Search Form

Click "filters" and then click the "Advanced" tab.

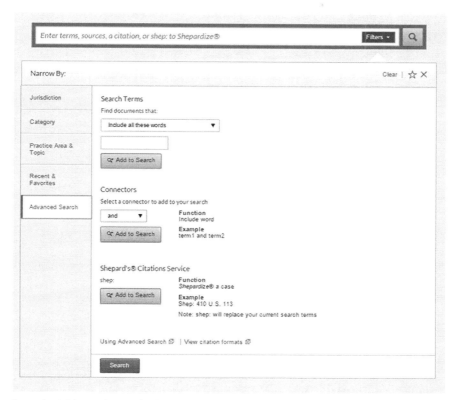

In addition to allowing you to craft a terms and connectors search in the search box, both Lexis and Westlaw offer "advanced" search options that allow you to craft a terms and connectors search with a form. See Figure 2-3. The benefit of search forms is that they can be easier than crafting your own terms and connectors search; the downside is that they may not allow the flexibility to search precisely what you want.

Chapter 3

Receiving Research Assignments and Gathering Facts

I. Introduction

Chapters 1 and 2 covered the research process and legal research techniques. This chapter focuses on techniques for gathering facts to inform your research.

A lawyer gets research projects in two ways: from a supervisor or directly from a client. This chapter will walk through both scenarios and provide tips for getting the most helpful information for your research. It also addresses briefly how to relay the results of your research to your supervisor or the client; knowing that will help you stay focused and keep your ultimate goals in mind.

II. Getting a Research Assignment from a Supervisor

Most law student interns and novice lawyers get their research assignments from more senior attorneys who are supervising their work. The senior attorney has communicated with the client, reviewed relevant papers, and reflected on those items to spot potential legal issues. Once the senior attorney has distilled the most likely legal issues, she will turn to the intern or new lawyer to perform the legal research. This part of the chapter assumes that you are that intern or new lawyer.

A. Learning About the Assignment
1. Take Notes

You will likely meet with a supervisor to receive a research assignment. Whenever you meet with a supervisor, bring a legal pad and take notes! You will find it very helpful to refer back to your notes as you work through the research process. Also, your notes can sometimes answer questions that develop a few days later and save you from returning to your supervisor to have her repeat information she has already given to you. Moreover, the scope of research projects frequently changes as time goes on. Your supervisor could receive additional information from the client, or she might discover a new case that impacts her initial determination of the likely legal issues. Always taking notes will help you stay on top of your research project as it grows and changes. Finally, even if you have the most perfect memory in the world and taking notes is not something that you have ever needed to do, take notes anyway. Nothing makes a supervisor more nervous than a junior attorney who doesn't take notes.

Be aware that the recommendation is to take your notes on a legal pad, not on your laptop. When you take notes on your laptop, the screen of your computer acts as a barrier between you and your supervisor. When you are trying to establish or maintain a good professional relationship, the details matter. You don't want to create even a vague feeling of a barrier between yourself and your supervisor. Moreover, your laptop can be distracting. For example, your email probably alerts you when you have new messages. Your supervisor will be able to tell if you are distracted by technology, even if only momentarily, and is unlikely to be impressed.

2. Ask Questions

During the course of your meeting, ask your supervisor if there are any documents or notes that you should review before beginning your research. These could include your supervisor's email correspondence with the client or notes on telephone calls with the client. It could include documents that the client has sent to your supervisor to review. If the client is a repeat client, it could also include items from your law office's client file.

You should also ask your supervisor logistical questions about the project. For example, how would she like you to convey the results of your research? She might want a full written memo, an email, or an in-person meeting. By when would she like the results? If she suggests a timeframe that is going to be difficult for you to meet given everything else on your plate, speak up right away. When you do, offer a realistic alternative target date. Finally, ask whether there are cost considerations that you should know about. Sometimes, a client strapped for cash will want to limit expenses. As a result, the client might prefer you to use print or free online resources over expensive online commercial legal research providers like Lexis and Westlaw.

3. Follow Up

After your meeting, review your meeting notes. Then, draft an email to your supervisor to confirm the substance of the assignment. Confirm the logistics of the assignment and ask any questions that you have developed since the meeting. Finally, ask your supervisor to let you know if you're missing anything. Your email might look something like this:

> Hi Suzanne,
>
> I am looking forward to getting started on my research for the Jeff Marlin case. To confirm, we are investigating whether Marlin has a theft of trade secrets case against his former employee, Doug Denton. I am researching whether Marlin took steps to preserve the secrecy of his winemaking process under North Dakota law. I'll have my memo to you by next Wednesday. Finally, do we have a copy of Marlin's winemaking manual? It might help for me to take a look at it as I conduct my research.
> Please let me know if I am missing anything.
>
> Best,
> Megan

Note that Megan first confirmed the substance of the assignment by summarizing the issue, whether Marlin took steps to preserve the secrecy of his winemaking process under North Dakota law. This allows Megan's supervisor to speak up if she wants Megan to focus on a different issue or another jurisdiction.

Megan then confirmed the logistics: Her response, in memo form, is due to her supervisor on Wednesday.

After confirming the logistics, Megan asked a question that she didn't think of during the meeting, whether there is additional material that might help her in her research.

Finally, note that Megan closed by asking her supervisor to respond to her only if Megan was missing something. This takes the burden off of Megan's supervisor to respond if Megan is getting everything right. While it might seem a small thing, you should avoid placing the burden on your supervisor to get back to you. "Let me know if I am missing anything" appears more confident and less needy than "Let me know if I have everything right."

B. Conducting Your Research

As you conduct your research, you will learn more about the law. And, as you learn more about the law, you will be better able to identify what additional facts you might need to conduct a complete analysis. Make note of all of the additional facts you might need and the additional questions you have as you conduct your research.

As you learn more about the law, you will also be able to generate additional search terms. Make a list of these terms and be sure to incorporate them into your research. This is where keeping a research log will be very helpful. With a log, you have a record of every step you took, and with what terms. Before you submit your final product to your supervisor, review your log to confirm that you have conducted a complete search.

Consider checking in with your supervisor periodically. This doesn't make sense for a three-hour project; it makes good sense for a multi-week project. Checking in with your supervisor will relieve her from having to reach out to you to confirm that the project is getting the attention it deserves. It also gives you a natural opportunity to do two things. First, you can let your supervisor know any additional categories of information that you need to complete the project. Second, you can alert your supervisor to any concerns you have about meeting your initial deadline. It's not a sin to miss a deadline; it is a sin not to tell your supervisor the moment you start to doubt your ability to meet it. When you do, be sure to include a realistic date by which you can complete the project.

C. Reporting Your Results

You will need to convey the results of your project to your supervisor. How you do that will depend on the medium that you were told to use to do so. Here are some tips for each:

Oral report. If you are reporting your results through a meeting, either in person or on the telephone, be sure to have your notes on research and analysis at your fingertips. Start the conversation by reminding your supervisor what she asked you to research, and give the bottom line answer with a very clear "yes" or "no." Starting with a clear answer up front immediately focuses your listener. It also allows her to not worry about listening for the ultimate answer as you talk; she already knows the answer, and she can now thoughtfully listen to the reasons that made you reach your conclusion.

When you explain why you reached your conclusion, identify the key rules and tell her how they apply to your client's situation. You might think of this as telling your supervisor the rules and application sections of a written memo; you won't provide the detailed explanation or rule proof unless your supervisor asks for more information.

Next, if there is information that you don't yet have that would impact your analysis, alert your supervisor to what that information is. If the list is long, you might consider having it in written form to give to your supervisor. Let her know how that information would impact your analysis.

Finally, be ready to field questions and take on follow-up work. To do so, you will want to have your research log, your key authorities, and your notes on the analysis. You will also want your legal pad and a pen.

Traditional memo. If you are reporting your results in a traditional memo, you will either email the memo to your supervisor, or you will bring it in hard copy to her office. If you are sending it via email, include a brief summary in the body of the email. Always start by reminding your supervisor what she asked you to research and give the bottom line answer. Then follow it up with a very short (one screen) summary of the reasons for your answer. You might also consider attaching the key authorities you relied on, with the critical passages highlighted.

If you are bringing your memo to your supervisor in hard copy, be prepared to also give an oral report and answer questions. See above for how to give an oral report. You might consider providing your supervisor with copies of the key authorities you relied on, with tabs on the pages with the most critical passages, and with those passages highlighted.

Email memo. If you are reporting your results in an email memo (usually more abbreviated than a traditional memo and sent in the body of an email), start by reminding your supervisor what she asked you to research, and provide your bottom line answer. Follow that with a short summary of reasons for your answer. Identify the rules and how they apply to your client's facts. Try to keep your answer to one screen. Again, you might consider attaching the key authorities you relied on, with the critical passages highlighted.

III. Getting a Research Assignment from a Client

You won't always have a supervisor who meets with the clients and determines what the legal issues are for you to research. Instead, it will be your job to meet with clients and spot the legal issues.

Table 3-1. Example Excerpted Written Chronology

Date	Event	Source
9/5/2005	Marlin discovers process for making Reserve Chardonnay	Marlin depo 1:11-17
10/4/2006	Denton hired as Williamsport Winery's head winemaker	Marlin depo 3:5-9, MAR-LIN00246
10/4/2006 – 6/18/2013	Denton participates in winemaking leadership and training academies	WW00345-456
7/11/2014	Denton quits to start his own winery	WW0022, Marlin depo 22:3-12
8/26/2015	Denton introduces his copycat wine; sells 50,000 cases	WW00486, DEN00014

A. The Client Meeting

1. Preparing for the Meeting

When a client contacts you with a problem, you'll likely set up an in-person meeting to discuss the problem and gather information. But during that initial contact, she'll usually give you some information on the problem that she is facing. If so, your first job is to start putting a chronology together. Putting the facts of your client's case in chronological order is the most effective way to learn the case and to understand how events relate to each other.

The chronology of a client's case has two parts: the written chronology and the document chronology. The written chronology has each fact, the date on which it occurred, and the source of the fact. You should keep updating the chronology throughout the case. A written chronology is particularly important if your client's problem develops into litigation. Not only does it give you a timeline of events; it also gives you a quick reference guide to the source of each fact. This will be very helpful when you need to write motions and briefs. An example of a written chronology appears in Table 3-1.

In the example written chronology, you can see the column for the date (or dates), a short summary of each fact, and the source. If the client's problem hasn't yet evolved into litigation, the most likely sources will be conversations with the client and the client's documents (including emails). If the problem evolves into litigation, some of the sources will likely be depositions and documents from the other side. In a deposition, a lawyer questions a witness in front of a court reporter to elicit testimony. In the example written chronology, you can see that the depositions are identified by the last name of the person who was deposed (the deponent), along with the page and line numbers of the testimony. So, "Marlin depo 1:11-17" is the Marlin deposition at page 1, lines 11 through 17. If the sources are documents from litigation, you will want to include the Bates number of the document. When parties collect and exchange documents in litigation, they index the documents with page numbers that have a prefix that helps to identify who the documents are from along with a page number. This is called a Bates number. In the example written chronology, some of the sources are documents, and the chronology lists the Bates number for each. For example, "WW00345-456" means that the documents are from Williamsport Winery, and the pages are 345 through 456.

In addition to the written chronology shown in Table 3-1, you will also want to start a document chronology. A document chronology is a collection of relevant documents—correspondence between the parties, relevant contracts, and any other relevant papers—all in chronological order. Like the written chronology, you should start your document chronology the moment you receive documents from your client, and you should keep it updated as the case progresses. When your document chronology gets too big to read through in one sitting, you can break it into two sets of documents: One with all of the documents from the case, and another one with only the most important documents from the case.

After you start your chronology, your second job is to conduct legal research in advance of the meeting. That early research will let you refresh yourself on the basics of the applicable law, prepare more effective questions, and have a better sense of what documents and other materials that you should ask to review.

On the day of the meeting, pay attention to the details from the moment you wake up in the morning. You want your client to have confidence in you, and you also want your client to be comfortable talking to you. As a result, select your clothing carefully. If your client is someone who is likely comfortable talking with a lawyer, like a local business owner, a suit is probably the appropriate selection. If your client is less likely to be comfortable talking with a lawyer, you might consider dressing in business casual.

When you arrive at the office, think about where you are going to have your meeting. If you are deeply involved in another case and have documents spread out in your office, try to meet in a conference room if you have one. If you do meet in your office, don't stay behind your desk, or the desk will act as a barrier between you and your client. Instead, come out from behind your desk and sit next to your client. This will help your client feel more at ease, especially if your client is someone who doesn't feel comfortable talking to a lawyer. The more comfortable your client is, the more likely you are to get all of the information you need to conduct your research.

2. Conducting the Meeting

Immediately before your client arrives, minimize any potential distractions. Turn off your smart phone, silence your email alert, and hold your office telephone calls.

When your client arrives, greet him and make some small talk. If small talk doesn't come naturally to you, prepare some questions in advance. "How was your drive?" "Can you believe all of this snow?"

Once you are settled, turn the conversation to your client's problem. While it can be tempting to start firing off a series of questions, it's best to ask the client to tell the entire story in his own words first. As the client is talking, listen actively. Nod your head and interject short responses that show you're following her story. Ask a question when you don't understand something. Take notes! And, just as when you are getting an assignment from a supervisor, take your notes on a legal pad instead of a laptop.

After your client is finished with his story, go back through it with him to confirm the details. As you do, intersperse your questions and requests for documents at the appropriate intervals. If your client is less sophisticated, try to use words like "papers" instead of "documents." If your client hasn't already told you what his ultimate goal is, be sure to ask.

Sometimes clients are afraid to share the "bad facts." There might be several reasons a client wants to withhold difficult information. The most typical are either that the client is embarrassed, or that the client is holding out the hope that you won't find out whatever it is and it will remain hidden forever. It is helpful to gently encourage your client to tell you everything, good and bad. You can help him with the bad facts that you know about; you can't help him if you're surprised by them at an inopportune moment in the case, like during settlement negotiations or trial. A less direct, and often helpful, way to elicit bad facts is to ask what the other side might say.

When you are finished confirming the story and asking your questions, ask your client one more time whether you're missing anything. Advise your client not to throw away anything having to do with the dispute—and this includes electronic materials, like emails.

After that, lay out your initial plan of action. If you can already determine what kind of issue or issues he is facing, let him know. Then, tell him what you're going to research. Confirm the materials that he has agreed to gather for you. Close the meeting by letting the client know when you will be back in touch.

3. Following Up After the Meeting

After the meeting, consider sending a brief follow up email. Open with something like "I appreciated the opportunity to meet with you today." Then, reiterate for your client the steps that you're taking and the steps that your client is taking. "As we discussed, I believe that your winemaking process is a trade secret under North Dakota law, but I would like to conduct additional research to confirm. You are going to gather all of your sales data for the past three years, and you are also going to send me a copy of your employee handbook." Close by telling your client when you plan to get back in touch with the results of your research.

B. Conducting Your Research

As you conduct your research, make a note of additional questions you develop. If you start to doubt your ability to be able to have an answer to your client by the date you initially proposed, let your client know right away. When you do, be sure to also let him know a realistic estimate of when you'll be able to get back to him.

C. Reporting Your Results

How you report your conclusion to your research depends on the client. Some clients will prefer an email or letter; others will want a telephone call or another in-person meeting.

1. Email or Letter

If your client prefers an email or letter, start with the bottom line answer. "After conducting research, I have determined that your winemaking process is a trade secret under North Dakota law."

Then, summarize the facts on which you have based your opinion. Be sure to tell your client that you have based your opinion on these facts; if you have omitted anything or gotten anything wrong, he needs to tell you because that could impact your opinion.

After that, give the reasons for your opinion. Lay out the legal rules and tell your client how they apply to his situation. Note that you will not include a lengthy explanation of the law or citations like you would in a traditional office memo.

Next, tell the client what his options are. He might take a wait-and-see approach; he might want to send the other side a letter asking for something (e.g., to quit making the wine); he might initiate a lawsuit; he might do something else altogether. Note which of the options will best meet the goal that he shared with you during your initial meeting.

Finally, if you or your client has remaining items to complete, like researching other legal issues or sending relevant documents, mention them. Then, let your client know when you will be back in touch to discuss the case.

2. Telephone Call or In-Person Meeting

Some clients will prefer you to communicate your results orally, either over the telephone or in person. If so, your meeting will be similar to the in-person meeting with a supervisor discussed above, with a few adjustments. First, remind the client what you researched and report your ultimate conclusion. Then, let the client know that your conclusion is based on the facts he communicated to you and those that you found in any documents he provided to you. List those facts, and ask whether you are missing anything or have misunderstood anything; if so, your opinion could change. Next, briefly explain to your client how the law applies to the facts of his case. As with the supervisor meeting, you should usually avoid in-depth explanation of the law with case or principle illustrations. If your client is another lawyer, however, you should be prepared to discuss the law in more detail if your client would like. Finally, end the meeting by laying out your client's options and identifying which most likely meets the goal he shared with you at your initial meeting.

IV. Conclusion

Fact gathering is an important part of any research project. The focus of this chapter has been the initial fact gathering. Note, however, that you will be gathering facts during the life of every case. The steps you learned here will help you in all phases of fact gathering. Remember that staying organized with tools like your notes, your research log, and your written and document chronology is critical to being an efficient and effective lawyer.

Chapter 4

Secondary Sources

I. Introduction

Previous chapters discussed the basics of how to effectively tackle a new research project. Much of the rest of this book will be devoted to locating and interpreting primary authority such as statutes, cases, and administrative regulations. However, as noted in Chapter 1, it is nearly always more effective to research in secondary sources before delving into primary sources. This chapter explains what secondary sources are, why they are valuable, and how to use them most effectively.

Secondary sources are publications that analyze, interpret, synthesize, or comment on the law. Virtually anyone who has conducted research in the past is already familiar with some types of secondary sources. For example, most researchers have used encyclopedias, dictionaries, and perhaps journal articles at some point. These same types of sources are available specifically in the field of law. Additional types of secondary sources are geared specifically toward legal practitioners, such as *American Law Reports* and legal practice guides. All of these types of secondary sources are discussed in this chapter.

Keep in mind that — unlike primary sources of law, such as statutes, cases, constitutions, and administrative regulation — secondary sources are not binding on the courts. This is because secondary sources are not, themselves, law. Instead, they are tools that lawyers and others use to understand the law. Typically, they are written by law professors, lawyers, and law students. Judges also can and do write secondary sources; note that when they do so, they are not writing as law-makers, but simply as legal experts.

While many secondary sources have a general, nationwide focus, some states also have their own state-specific secondary sources. For example, California lawyers have access to legal encyclopedias, practice guides, and other materials geared specifically toward California law. Very few secondary sources are written specifically for the state of North Dakota. Therefore, most of the sources in

this chapter have a more general orientation for use by lawyers in any jurisdiction. Nonetheless, many general secondary sources provide information on
and citations to North Dakota state law. Even where a secondary source does
not specifically reference North Dakota, it may be useful as a starting point in
understanding the basic contours of a given law and in developing search terms
that will aid you in researching in primary sources.

II. Why Use Secondary Sources?

A. Usefulness of Secondary Sources

All expert legal researchers advise novices to begin their research with secondary sources. Secondary sources provide a wealth of valuable information
about the law and are typically better indexed and easier to use than primary
sources. Even experienced legal researchers can often benefit from beginning
with secondary sources, particularly when researching a new or unfamiliar
legal topic. Secondary sources can also make research in primary sources more
efficient and cost-effective by identifying relevant citations in primary sources.
To better understand the value of secondary sources, imagine that legal research
is like taking a trip to a destination that you've never been. Going straight to
primary sources is akin to just jumping in the car and driving around aimlessly,
hoping you eventually get to your destination; starting with secondary sources
is like consulting a map or asking a friend for directions.

Secondary sources are valuable in several key ways, depending on the source
you use. First, secondary sources allow you to develop a basic understanding
of the law in question before turning to primary sources. Most secondary
sources are written in fairly plain language, making them quicker and easier
to understand than many statutes, cases, and regulations. They also often allow
you to get a more holistic picture of the law; in other words, they show where
your particular issue fits within the greater context of the subject in question.
Additionally, they can help you to understand complex legal terminology and
to develop good search terms that you might then use in researching primary
sources.

Another valuable use of secondary sources is as a finding tool for primary
authority. Most secondary sources contain a great number of footnotes; these
footnotes provide citations to the primary authority from which the material
was derived. Therefore, looking at the footnotes in a secondary source will
often guide you fairly quickly and directly to important statutes, cases, and
regulations. Many secondary sources also have citations to other secondary

sources that can provide you with more detailed information on the law and more footnotes to explore.

Sometimes, secondary sources may even be of value as persuasive authority that you will want to present to the court. While in most instances it is not good practice to cite to secondary sources, there are a few exceptions to this general rule. For example, if no law exists on a particular issue in your jurisdiction, then you might cite to a secondary source that summarizes what other jurisdictions are doing. If you would like to argue for a change in the law, then secondary sources may help to provide arguments for why the law should be changed or why the current law should be interpreted one way rather than another.

B. Persuasiveness of Secondary Sources

When you do decide to cite to a secondary source, however, do not forget that secondary sources are not binding; they are persuasive authority only. Further, not all secondary sources are considered equally persuasive. The persuasive value of a secondary source is heavily dependent on four characteristics: who wrote it, the depth in which it covers a given topic, the level at which it has been cited in the past, and when it was published.

First, the most authoritative secondary sources are those published by prominent scholars, judges, and attorneys. For example, restatements,[1] which are written by the prestigious American Law Institute, are probably the most persuasive secondary source; in fact, many courts adopt common law for their jurisdiction directly from the Restatements. Law review articles and treatises written by well known authors may also be very persuasive, but you need to be a bit more careful with these as the very same type of sources may carry far less weight if the author is not prominent.

Next, secondary sources that cover a particular topic in depth, especially when that coverage is jurisdiction-specific, carry greater weight than those that are more general. Thus, a treatise or law review article will typically be considered more persuasive than a legal encyclopedia or a dictionary.

Third, a secondary source is usually considered more persuasive if it has been cited often. This is especially true if citations to the source were in judicial opinions, although a piece that is cited heavily in other secondary sources may also be persuasive.

---

1. Restatements will be discussed in greater detail in Part III.F.

Fourth, the timing of publication of a secondary source may also be important. As with primary sources, in most instances, the more recently a source has been published, the better.

III. Common Secondary Sources and How to Research Them

A wide variety of secondary sources is available. Some are particularly valuable at the very beginning of the research process while others are better for gaining more in-depth knowledge once you have a handle on the basic concepts. This part of the chapter describes some of the most common secondary sources and explains how to research them.

A. Legal Dictionaries

Legal dictionaries provide definitions of common legal terminology. Legal dictionaries are particularly valuable for looking up words and phrases that may have a different meaning in legal documents than they do in daily usage. Some legal dictionaries also include citations to the source from where the definition was derived.

The most widely used legal dictionary is *Black's Law Dictionary*. It is available both in print and on Westlaw. Another popular legal dictionary is *Ballantine's Law Dictionary*, which is available on Lexis. Keep in mind that, while a legal dictionary may help you to understand an unfamiliar legal term, the dictionary definition itself is not the law and should not be cited as though it were authoritative. On occasion, a court may cite to a legal dictionary; on those occasions, the legal researcher should cite the court's opinion, not the dictionary.

B. Legal Encyclopedias

1. Overview

Legal encyclopedias are much like ordinary encyclopedias except that they solely address legal topics. They provide a broad overview of a given topic as well as some citations to primary sources and other secondary sources. Legal encyclopedias are most useful at the beginning of the research process, especially when researching a new or unfamiliar topic, because they cover the law at a general level, as opposed to analyzing specifics in depth. They are also fairly easy to browse; once you find a specific entry that is helpful, you can look at the entries on the surrounding pages to find other, related information. The most commonly used legal encyclopedias on the market are *American Jurisprudence 2d* (Am. Jur. 2d) and *Corpus Juris Secundum* (C.J.S.).

Most legal encyclopedias, including both Am. Jur. 2d and C.J.S. are written from a national perspective; thus, they do not typically cover the particular laws of individual states, although they may cite to primary sources in a variety of states. On occasion, however, specific states may be discussed to highlight variations in the law across jurisdictions. Additionally, some state-specific legal encyclopedias exist for larger states (e.g., California, Ohio, and Florida); however, many states, including North Dakota, do not have their own legal encyclopedias.

2. Researching Legal Encyclopedias

Am. Jur. 2d and C.J.S. are available in print and online; Am. Jur. 2d is available on Lexis and Westlaw, but C.J.S. is available only on Westlaw.

Although you can conduct full-text searches in the online versions of Am. Jur. 2d and C.J.S., it is often more effective to begin with the table of contents or the index. Most legal encyclopedias are organized alphabetically by main topic, with sub-topics included under the main topic heading. You may begin by browsing the table of contents or, if you are not sure under which main heading your issue would fall, searching the index. Make sure to use multiple search terms to ensure that you are finding the most pertinent topics and sub-topics.

Once you have located a pertinent topic or sub-topic, look at where the topic starts in the encyclopedia. This section will provide you with a summary of what is covered under that topic. For example, Figure 4-1 shows a screen shot of part of the summary found at the beginning of the Am. Jur. 2d topic "Adoption."

Additionally, read whichever sub-topic seems most useful carefully, but don't forget to browse the other sub-topics under your main topic as they may provide useful information as well. As you read the relevant entries, be sure to jot down citations to primary and secondary sources that seem like they might be useful as well as any legal terminology that you might come across that will help you develop search terms for other sources. Finally, if using an online version of the encyclopedias, ensure that your research is up-to-date by using Shepard's or KeyCite. If you are using a print version, check the pocket part in the volume in which your topic appears.

Figure 4-1. Summary at the Beginning of the Am. Jur. 2d Topic "Adoption"

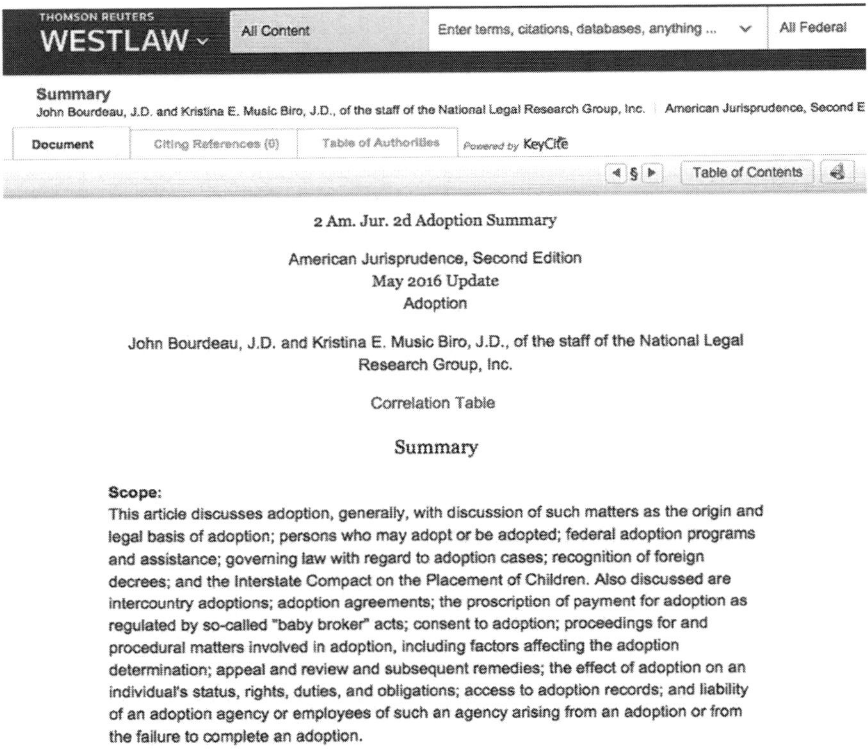

THOMSON REUTERS WESTLAW | All Content | Enter terms, citations, databases, anything ... | All Federal

Summary
John Bourdeau, J.D. and Kristina E. Music Biro, J.D., of the staff of the National Legal Research Group, Inc. | American Jurisprudence, Second E

Document | Citing References (0) | Table of Authorities | Powered by KeyCite

§ | Table of Contents

2 Am. Jur. 2d Adoption Summary

American Jurisprudence, Second Edition
May 2016 Update
Adoption

John Bourdeau, J.D. and Kristina E. Music Biro, J.D., of the staff of the National Legal Research Group, Inc.

Correlation Table

Summary

Scope:
This article discusses adoption, generally, with discussion of such matters as the origin and legal basis of adoption; persons who may adopt or be adopted; federal adoption programs and assistance; governing law with regard to adoption cases; recognition of foreign decrees; and the Interstate Compact on the Placement of Children. Also discussed are intercountry adoptions; adoption agreements; the proscription of payment for adoption as regulated by so-called "baby broker" acts; consent to adoption; proceedings for and procedural matters involved in adoption, including factors affecting the adoption determination; appeal and review and subsequent remedies; the effect of adoption on an individual's status, rights, duties, and obligations; access to adoption records; and liability of an adoption agency or employees of such an agency arising from an adoption or from the failure to complete an adoption.

Source: Westlaw. Reprinted with permission from Thomson Reuters.

C. Treatises

1. Overview

Treatises are scholarly publications that address one particular area of law in detail. They are typically written by legal scholars, and they provide in-depth analyses, including citations to primary sources, on the legal topic in question. They may be published as a single volume or in a multi-volume set, and may be hardbound or published in "looseleaf" format.[2] Hardbound treatises

2. Looseleaf treatises should not be confused with looseleaf services, which are discussed in III.G.2 of this chapter.

are typically updated by pocket parts; looseleaf treatises are published in ringed binders, with removable pages, and are updated when pages are added or removed at the instruction of the publisher.[3] However, not every treatise is updated, so you must evaluate each individual treatise carefully to ensure that its content is current.

Treatises are much more thorough than legal encyclopedias and are an excellent choice when you understand the basic contours of your topic but need to gain a deeper understanding of the laws and rules that apply. The persuasive value of a given treatise depends heavily on its reputation, determined by such factors as the author's reputation and the frequency with which the treatise has been cited by the courts and others. When you are new to a topic, it is worth asking a law librarian or, at the very least, doing a Google search, to determine which treatises are considered the "best" in a given topic area.

2. Researching Treatises

Unlike many legal sources, treatises are not yet widely available online. This means you should anticipate that you may need to consult print publications in order to get the widest selection.

Although not all treatises are identical, most will include a table of contents as well as an index. Those are the best places to start in locating the portion of the treatise that is most pertinent to your research topic. Once you find a relevant section, read it thoroughly. Most treatises are heavily footnoted, so, as you read, be sure to take notes on citations to relevant primary and secondary authority. As with legal encyclopedias, it is also often worthwhile to browse the sections immediately preceding and following the section that you find most useful. As always, you should ensure that your research is up-to-date by checking the pocket parts or new looseleaf pages where applicable.

Even though you may have to rely on print treatises, note that both Lexis and Westlaw have some treatises available, particularly some of the more famous ones in popular subject areas. You should consult the secondary source and subject-area databases in those services to see which treatises are available. When using a treatise on Lexis or Westlaw, full-text searching will be available, although where those services also include the table of contents and indexes, those are still the best places to start. Make sure that you check the source in-

---

3. New pages are often in a different color than the other pages to make the updates more obvious to the researcher.

formation for the treatise so that you are aware of when it was last updated. Some treatises that are still regularly updated in print are not updated as often in the online services.

Other services, such as Bloomberg BNA, may also provide access to treatises. The same principles applied in searching Lexis and Westlaw can be adapted to other such services.

D. *American Law Reports* (A.L.R.) Annotations

1. Overview

The *American Law Reports* (A.L.R.) collects long, detailed essays, previously called "annotations" and now called "articles," on very particular legal issues.[4] A.L.R.s typically focus on areas of controversial or emerging law. While A.L.R.s are not written for all topics, an A.L.R. on the specific topic you are researching can be an extremely valuable resource. A.L.R. annotations are extensively footnoted and include references to primary authority from all fifty states (if applicable), federal law (again, if applicable), and other secondary sources. Because A.L.R. annotations are rather narrow, you will typically want to consult this source a little later in your secondary source research, once you have a somewhat solid understanding of your legal issue and are ready to delve deeper.

Each annotation is accompanied by a brief description of the content of the annotation; a very general table of contents; an article outline that acts as a more substantial table of contents; an index; a table of cases, laws, and rules; and a list of references to other secondary sources. The table of cases, laws, and rules is organized first by federal jurisdiction and then alphabetically state-by-state, where applicable state materials exist.[5]

Due to the number of volumes and the length of time A.L.R.s have been published, there are now several different "series" of A.L.R.s. The first two series, A.L.R. and A.L.R.2d as well as some volumes in A.L.R.3d covered both federal and state law. Federal law was then moved into separate volumes, which now include A.L.R. Fed, A.L.R. Fed. 2d. and A.L.R. Fed. 3d. The later volumes

---

4. Note that A.L.R.s also publish some cases; the publisher selects a case that exemplifies the basic topic or controversy that the annotation covers. However, the primary value of A.L.R.s is in the annotations and their accompanying materials, so that is what this section of the chapter discusses.

5. One instance where you might use an A.L.R. early in your research is to check this table in an annotation that seems exactly on point. It might list North Dakota authority, essentially doing your research for you.

of A.L.R.3d as well as A.L.R.4th, A.L.R.5th, A.L.R.6th, and A.L.R.7th focus solely on state law.

2. Researching A.L.R. Annotations

A.L.R.s are available both in print and online in Lexis and Westlaw. If researching in print, the easiest way to find relevant annotations is via the A.L.R. Index to Annotations, which, like other indexes, is organized alphabetically by key words and phrases. There is also a "Table of Laws, Rules, and Regulations," located at the back of the index, which may be helpful if you are beginning your research with a specific primary authority, such as a statute, in mind. Using this table, you can look up a citation to primary authority and find out any annotations that mention the authority. Finally, there is an A.L.R. Digest, which is organized by topic and sub-topic; however, the A.L.R. Index is generally somewhat easier to use.

When researching in print A.L.R.s, it is often more efficient to ensure that any relevant annotations you find are up-to-date before digging into them too deeply. You don't want to read an annotation only to discover that a case has since come down in your jurisdiction that makes the annotation irrelevant for your purposes. Both the A.L.R. Index and the A.L.R. Digest, as well as individual volumes, are updated by pocket parts, so be sure to check these to ensure that you have the most up-to-date information. Additionally, the A.L.R. Index includes an "Annotation History Table," which can be helpful in determining whether an older annotation has been superseded by a more recent one.

A.L.R.s are also available on Lexis and Westlaw. Try searching for key words or phrases in the index or in the full text of the annotations. The databases on Lexis and Westlaw are updated weekly. You can also use the Shepard's and KeyCite features to ensure that your research is up-to-date.

Once you have found a relevant annotation, read the introductory material carefully to ensure that it is on point. You may want to skip to the table of cases and statutes accompanying the annotation to see if anything from North Dakota has been cited. Even if it hasn't, the annotation may still be worth looking at to learn more about the topic and to find citations to persuasive primary authority, such as cases and statutes in nearby jurisdictions. The index near the beginning of the annotation may lead to the particular aspects of your legal issue that you would like to learn more about.

Figure 4-2 provides a screen shot from Lexis showing an excerpt from the table of cases and statutes for an A.L.R.4th annotation entitled, "Liability for Personal Injury or Death Caused by Trespassing or Intruding Livestock." This excerpt shows one case in North Dakota on this topic.

**Figure 4-2. Excerpt from the Table of Cases and
Statutes for an A.L.R.4th Annotation**

MONTANA

Hughey v Fergus County (1934) 98 Mont 98, 37 P2d 1035 (recognizing rule)

NEW YORK

Hollenbeck v Johnson (1894) 79 Hun 499, 29 NYS 945 (by implication)
Kinmouth v McDougall (1892, Sup) 19 NYS 771, affd 139 NY 612, 35 NE 204
Malone v Knowlton (1891, Sup) 15 NYS 506
Marsh v Hand (1890) 120 NY 315, 24 NE 463 (recognizing rule)
Rogers v Rogers (1887, Sup) 4 NYSR 373
Van Leuven v Lyke (1848) 1 NY 515 (recognizing rule)
Warsevecz v Mills (1939) 258 App Div 846, 15 NYS2d 687 (by implication)

NORTH DAKOTA

Peterson v Conlan (1909) 18 ND 205, 119 NW 367

OHIO

Bolton v Barkhurst (1973, Wood Co) 40 Ohio App 2d 353, 69 Ohio Ops 2d 316, 319 NE2d 376 (recognizing rule)
Nixon v Harris (1968) 15 Ohio St 2d 105, 44 Ohio Ops 2d 78, 238 NE2d 785
Petit v Hudson (1862) 2 Ohio Dec Reprint 660, 4 West L Month 434 (also stating that under common law of England and c

Source: Lexis Advance. Reprinted with permission from Reed Elsevier.

E. Legal Periodicals

A variety of law reviews,[6] magazines, and newspapers are dedicated to the law and legal topics; collectively, these are known as "legal periodicals." For most legal researchers, the most valuable of these sources will be law reviews, although bar journals and newspapers may also be helpful for staying up-to-date on a state's legal community and laws.

1. Law Review Articles

a. Overview

The most widely used and comprehensive of legal periodicals are law review articles. Law review articles are long (usually), scholarly pieces that deal with a particular topic in depth. Law review articles are heavily footnoted. Thus, their value is not only in the scholarly discussion and analysis of a particular topic but also in the large number of references to other primary and secondary sources.

Most law reviews are edited and published by student organizations at law schools around the country, although a few are edited and published by other legal organizations. Some law reviews, such as the *Harvard Law Review*, have broad coverage, containing articles on a virtually limitless set of legal topics. Others are more narrowly focused on a particular area of law, typically indicated

---

6. Law reviews are also sometimes referred to as law journals.

by the title of the journal. For example, the *Berkeley Journal of Employment & Labor Law* is dedicated to publishing scholarship in the areas of employment and labor law. The University of North Dakota School of Law currently publishes two different law reviews. The *North Dakota Law Review* is a traditional, broadly focused law review. The *Journal of Law and Interdisciplinary Studies* is an online-only journal publishing essays and responses in areas where legal study overlaps with other areas of study, such as psychology or sociology.

Law review articles vary greatly in quality, and you should be sure to evaluate both the author and the publication in which the article appears. Most law review articles are written by law professors and practitioners such as judges, lawyers, and policy analysts. However, a sizeable number of articles are written by students; student articles are usually referred to as "notes" or "comments." In general, the more prestigious the author and publication, the more weight an article will hold. Even so, don't overlook student articles entirely; many of them are quite well researched and well written. Even if they are not considered as persuasive as other articles, they will still have a wealth of footnotes to help you locate other materials.

To evaluate the persuasiveness of a given article, look at how often the article has been cited; an article with a large number of citations is likely considered by the scholarly community to be more authoritative than an article on a similar topic with fewer citations. Also consider the age of the publication, as very recent articles might contain important updates and analysis, even though they haven't been in print long enough to garner a large number of citations.

b. Researching Law Review Articles

Although it is possible to research in individual law reviews, that is virtually never the most effective method of finding pertinent law review articles. Thus, this section discusses finding articles using tools that collect or index articles from many different law reviews. Further, while law reviews are available both in print and online, online research is by far the preferable method; in fact, more and more law libraries are trimming their print collections in this area due to cost and space constraints. Therefore, this section discusses only online searching.

Lexis and Westlaw both have databases containing most major law reviews. Lexis has a database for "Secondary Materials"; after completing a search in this database, you can click a link on the side of the page to narrow your search to "Law Reviews and Journals." On Westlaw, first click on the tab in the "Browse" area labeled "Secondary Sources" and then the "Law Reviews and Journals" database.

Coverage for each law review included in the databases varies, although, generally speaking, articles from at least the past twenty to twenty-five years are included. These databases are easily searched by keyword. HeinOnline also contains a huge number of law reviews, in PDF format, and its time coverage is far wider; for many law reviews, coverage goes all the way back to the first issue. However, its searching capabilities are not as advanced as Lexis and Westlaw, so HeinOnline is often more easily used when you have already obtained a citation to a specific article elsewhere.

Additionally, many law libraries subscribe to online indexes[7] that can be searched by topic or author to find relevant law review articles. Some indexes also provide the ability to search by case name or statute. The most well known online indexes are the *Index to Legal Periodicals and Books* and *LegalTrac* (also known as the *Current Law Index* or *Legal Resource Index*). It is typically easiest to search these indexes in their stand-alone subscription formats. However, there is some availability of *LegalTrac* on Lexis and Westlaw; on both services, it is known by its alternate name, *Legal Resource Index*. On Lexis, click on "Browse" and then "Sources." Beneath the "Sources" link, a box will appear allowing you to search for a database; type in "Legal Resource Index" there. On Westlaw, click on "Secondary Sources." At the right, under the "Tools & Resources" heading, you will see a link to the Legal Resource Index.

Some law reviews publish their articles online, typically from the most recent issues. This means a Google or Google Scholar search may also prove profitable. Additionally, even if the full text of the article is not available online, such a search might lead to a citation so that you could retrieve the article from one of the online services listed above.

2. Bar Journals and Newspapers

Bar journals typically have much more abbreviated coverage than law reviews and are best for keeping up with new developments in the law in a particular state. Most bar associations publish their own bar journals, which may include such information as articles on practice, developments in the state, reports on attorneys who have been disciplined, and upcoming events.

The State Bar Association of North Dakota (SBAND) publishes a bar journal called *The Gavel*, which is published quarterly. Current and past versions back to 2005 can be accessed on the SBAND website.[8] Additionally, some state law

---

7. These indexes are available both in print and online, but the online version is typically easier to use, and many law libraries may not subscribe to the print version.

8. The address is www.sband.org.

libraries, including the Thormodsgard Law Library at University of North Dakota, have subscriptions. While there is not a particularly efficient way to search *The Gavel*, you may be able to find relevant articles via Google or from references in law review articles.

Some bar associations or private publishers also publish state- or even city-specific legal newspapers that contain material similar to that included in bar journals. Currently, there are no such publications in North Dakota.

F. Restatements

1. Overview

Restatements are long works that synthesize the common law. Their purpose is to help pull together the common law from various jurisdictions and "restate" it in a more rule-like format. Written by esteemed scholars for the American Law Institute, restatements are one of the most authoritative secondary sources available to the legal researcher. Much of the time, the restated "rule" is based on the rule that has been adopted by the majority of courts nationwide, with additional discussion of significant minority interpretations. However, when the authors deem the minority rule the better one, the synthesized rule will be based on that minority interpretation instead.

Restatements exist for a limited number of topics. Table 4-1 lists those topics for which there are restatements.[9] A restatement for your research topic, however, can be an extremely helpful source. Restatements provide not only the rule but also comments discussing what the rule means, illustrations of how it works in practice, and, in newer restatements, notes explaining how the rule was created and providing citations to primary and secondary sources. Keep in mind, though, that although restatements resemble statutes in certain respects, they are not actually law unless adopted in a given jurisdiction.

2. Researching Restatements

Restatements are available both in print and online in Lexis and Westlaw. Each restatement has a table of contents and an index that will assist you in finding relevant sections. Typically, you will want to read more than one section of the restatement. Look for the one that seems the most pertinent, but also read those located near it as they will typically explain related material that

---

9. Additionally, restatements are designated with a "series" number when newer versions are published. So, for example, there is a *Restatement (First) of Contracts* and a *Restatement (Second) of Contracts*.

Table 4-1. Topics For Which There Are Restatements

Agency

Conflict of Laws

Contracts

Foreign Relations

Judgments

Law Governing Lawyers

Property (additional, more specialized, restatements under this topic include: Donative Transfers, Landlord and Tenant, Mortgages, Servitudes, and Wills & Other Donative Transfers)

Restitution

Security

Suretyship & Guaranty

Torts (additional, more specialized, restatements under this topic include: Apportionment of Liability, Physical and Emotional Harm, and Products Liability)

Trusts (an additional, more specialized, restatement under this topic is Prudent Investor Rule).

Unfair Competition

may also be relevant. Also, be sure to look over the commentary and illustrations to get a fuller picture of the rule.

You will also want to research how the restatement has been treated in your jurisdiction. This means checking for cases that have cited to the restatement. In print, you can use the Appendix volumes accompanying the regular restatement volumes to look for citing cases; be sure to check the pocket parts to ensure that you have the most up-to-date information. Online, Lexis and Westlaw also provide links to case citations for each restatement, and you can use Shepard's and KeyCite. Finally, to fully ensure that your research is comprehensive, you may want to conduct a case search looking for references to the restatement in your jurisdiction, using the techniques discussed in Chapter 11, Cases.

G. Other Secondary Sources

1. Continuing Legal Education Materials

In most states, attorneys are required to take a certain number of continuing education classes each year in order to maintain their law licenses and keep up with new developments in the law and legal ethics. Continuing legal education materials are the materials that are published (typically handouts) in conjunction with such classes.

Some major CLE organizations publish their materials online. Check the American Law Institute–American Bar Association (ALI-ABA); the American Bar Association (ABA); and the Practising Law Institute (PLI) websites. Lexis and Westlaw also publish some CLE materials. Some law libraries collect them as well; check your library's catalog to see what's available in your location.

2. Looseleaf Services

Looseleaf services are somewhat similar to treatises in terms of providing in-depth coverage on a particular area of law; however, unlike treatises, looseleafs compile the main statutes and rules that govern a particular area of law and are geared more obviously toward practitioners. In spite of including this primary authority, looseleafs are most useful as a secondary source, providing citations to cases and administrative opinions as well as analysis aimed at lawyers practicing in that area of law. In print, looseleafs are held together in binders. When a new development in the law occurs, a library carrying a looseleaf service will receive updated pages on a pre-determined schedule (typically monthly or quarterly) to insert into the books. Sometimes these pages are additions; sometimes they replace other pages that have become irrelevant, which are simultaneously removed. Each looseleaf is different, so when researching in print, consult the "how to use" section of the looseleaf.

While some looseleaf services are available on Lexis and Westlaw, more are available through databases maintained by their publishers. The main looseleaf publishers are Bloomberg BNA, Commerce Clearing House (C.C.H.), and Research Institute of America (R.I.A.). Check with your local library to determine if it has a subscription to any of these databases.

3. Practice Guides, Forms, and Jury Instructions

Practice guides provide detailed overviews of specific areas of law geared particularly toward practicing attorneys. Like treatises, practice guides can be single- or multi-volume and most are updated regularly; their main difference from treatises is the specific orientation toward practicing attorneys. This means, in part, that these guides include practice-related tools such as step-by-step instructions and sample documents.

The most useful practice guides are those that are specific to a particular jurisdiction. Although no North Dakota-specific practice guides are currently on the market, looking for a general practice guide by topic may still be a useful starting point. For example, you might look for a practice guide either in a library catalog or online on Lexis or Westlaw, just to give yourself a general idea of how a particular type of case might be presented. Just ensure that you double-check anything you find against North Dakota law.

Forms and jury instructions are model legal documents that assist practitioners. Forms may be found individually or in "formbooks," collecting multiple types of forms together. Some examples of forms are (1) worksheets for calculating the appropriate amount of child support or (2) a list of questions that must be answered and submitted to a court for a person to qualify to have a prior crime expunged from his or her record.

Jury instructions are the instructions given to a jury about how it must consider during its deliberation the information provided at trial. Providing appropriate jury instructions is extremely important; a case can turn as much on how the jury evaluates evidence as on the evidence that is provided. Model jury instructions provide a starting point for litigators seeking to ensure that they are able to build a successful case and give the jury instructions that are best for their clients.

Many books containing forms and jury instructions also provide annotations explaining the primary source from which the language or principles in the forms or jury instructions was derived.

State-specific forms and jury instructions can often be found for free online. For example, the State Bar Association of North Dakota (SBAND) has a webpage on which pattern jury instructions for both civil and criminal cases are published. To locate them, click on "Pattern Jury Instructions" from the SBAND home page. Performing a Google search for state-specific forms can also be helpful. The North Dakota official government website has a page listing some e-forms,[10] and individual agencies may also have forms that can be downloaded.

For more general materials, Lexis and Westlaw have various databases for forms and jury instructions. Additionally, many practice guides include similar materials.

---

10. *See* http://www.nd.gov/eforms/.

4. Library Research Guides

Library research guides are often overlooked but extremely valuable resources for figuring out what primary and secondary sources are available and how to access them. Law libraries and non-profit agencies across the country publish such guides, and most publish the guides online for free. Given the huge variety of sources available in different states, a guide can help you narrow down the particular resources available in your state. A large variety of subject-specific guides are also available, on everything from Administrative Law to Water Law. Such guides will typically provide a list of the sources available and how to locate them; many also include a brief overview of the type of law in question.

The easiest way to find a good research guide is to simply perform a Google-type search on your topic and include "research guide" or "legal research guide" in the search. Additionally, some larger law libraries have particularly comprehensive and easy-to-use collections. For example, the Georgetown Law Library provides a searchable collection of legal research guides on a large variety of topics.[11] That library has a guide entitled "North Dakota Resources," which summarizes many of the primary sources discussed later in this book.

---

11. *See* https://www.law.georgetown.edu/library/research/guides/.

Chapter 5

Constitutional Law

I. The Role of State Constitutions in the U.S. Legal System

The following chapters explain how to research the major sources of North Dakota state law, such as statutes, cases, and administrative rules. This chapter explores the source of the state's power to make such laws and to structure the state government — the state constitution.

State constitutions play an important role in the legislative system of the United States. Under the Tenth Amendment to the United States Constitution, "[t]he powers not delegated to the United States by the Constitution, nor prohibited by it to the States, are reserved to the States respectively, or to the people."[1] This amendment ensures that states have the right to create and interpret their own constitutions and other laws, provided they do not conflict with federal law.

State constitutions do not follow any uniform structure, and different states make different choices in terms of what is and is not included in the state constitution. For example, ten states now explicitly address the right to privacy in their constitutions, while the other forty states do not. State constitutions vary significantly in areas affecting everything from gun control to health care reform to education funding.

However, there are some similarities across state constitutions. First, state constitutions are typically longer and more detailed than the United States Constitution. For example, the North Dakota State Constitution has about 18,900 words compared to about 8,700 words for the U.S. Constitution. Second, state constitutions typically include far more detail than the federal constitution and cover many more areas of concern, including, for example, such matters

---

1. U.S. Const. Amend. X.

as public education and marriage. Finally, state constitutions are typically much easier to amend than the federal constitution is. This combination of detail and ease of amendment can lead some state constitutions to grow long and cluttered and to cover areas that are more traditionally governed by statute.

When researching state constitutional law, keep in mind that the federal constitution acts as a "floor" rather than a "ceiling" in terms of the rights that the states may provide to citizens. That is, while state constitutions may not be less protective of individual rights than the federal constitution, they may be, and often are, *more* protective of individual rights. So long as there is no conflict with federal law, states have the ultimate authority to interpret their own constitutions. Under the doctrine of preemption, however, federal law will prevail when there is a conflict.

II. The North Dakota Constitution: Background and History

The North Dakota State Constitution is the main governing document of the state. Similar to the United States Constitution, it includes a declaration of rights (analogous to the U.S. Constitution's Bill of Rights) as well as articles governing the power of the legislative, executive, and judicial branches and other matters. However, unlike the U.S. Constitution, there is no separate list of amendments in the North Dakota constitution; instead, amendments are directly incorporated into the relevant article.

The North Dakota Constitution was ratified by voters on October 1, 1889, a month before North Dakota was officially granted statehood on November 2, 1889. Earlier that year, the United States Congress had passed the Enabling Act of February 2, 1889, which authorized the pending statehood as well as a state Constitutional Convention. The Constitutional Convention opened on July 4 of that year and consisted of seventy-five delegates, mostly farmers and lawyers representing the eastern portion of the state.

According to the State Historical Society of North Dakota,[2] the Convention inspired few controversies. Among the issues that caused more extensive debate were women's suffrage, prohibition, and the location of public institutions. In fact, prohibition was so controversial that it was actually presented to the voters separately, at the same time as the constitution, to ensure that if it did

---

2. *See* http://history.nd.gov/index.html.

not pass, the rest of the document would still survive.[3] As enacted, the constitution included a preamble, twenty articles divided into 217 sections, and twenty-six separate transitional sections dealing with North Dakota's conversion from territory to state.

Since that time, the North Dakota Constitution has been amended many times. It can be amended in one of three ways: legislatively referred amendments;[4] constitutional convention;[5] and, since 1914, initiated constitutional amendments.[6] New amendments are submitted directly to the electorate and are approved if they garner a majority of the votes. As of the 2014 election, the North Dakota Constitution has been amended over 150 times since its adoption. Contrast this with the U.S. Constitution, which, since its enactment in 1789 has been amended only twenty-seven times, including the adoption of the Bill of Rights.

Today, the North Dakota Constitution includes a preamble, thirteen articles, and a transition schedule, which provides for publication and dissemination of new versions of the Constitution after amendments.

For a list of North Dakota's constitutional articles, see Table 5-1.

III. Researching North Dakota Constitutional Issues

How you approach researching the North Dakota Constitution depends on both the reasons for your research and the information with which you begin. For example, if you already know that a constitutional provision exists, you might go straight to the constitution itself. If you aren't sure whether a state constitutional provision is on point, it will often be more efficient to start in

---

3. Prohibition did pass and was included in the original constitution; however, it was repealed in 1932.

4. A legislatively referred amendment is an amendment that was approved by the state legislature before being put on the ballot for a direct vote by the electorate. When the legislature proposes a constitutional amendment for voter consideration, it does so as a "Resolution," a form of legislative action that does not have the effect of law and also covers such areas as expressing legislative opinions or requesting actions.

5. Other than its original constitutional convention, convened at the beginning of its statehood, North Dakota has only had one other constitutional convention, in the 1971–72 legislative year. The new constitution proposed at the convention was defeated by the voters at a special election held on April 28, 1972.

6. Initiated constitutional amendments refer to amendments put forth directly by voters via the initiative process. For more information on the initiative process, see Chapter 13.

Table 5-1. Articles in the North Dakota Constitution

Preamble

Article I: Declaration of Rights

Article II: Elective Franchise

Article III: Powers Reserved to the People

Article IV: Legislative Branch

Article V: Executive Branch

Article VI: Judicial Branch

Article VII: Political Subdivisions

Article VIII: Education

Article IX: Trust Lands

Article X: Finance and Public Debt

Article XI: General Provisions

Article XII: Corporations Other Than Municipal

Article XIII: Compact With The United States

other sources. The main consideration to keep in mind is that, when conducting legal research on any topic, you should always pay attention to whether the topic is governed by any constitutional provision. Remember that, barring any conflict with federal law, the state constitution is the highest legal authority in the state, so if a constitutional provision governs your topic, you need to know about it and understand it.

Several efficient strategies for researching North Dakota constitutional issues are explained next. Many of these strategies rely on techniques discussed in other chapters; to avoid excessive repetition, strategies and sources that are covered elsewhere will be summarized here but not discussed in full detail. You should check other relevant chapters for further details on the techniques and sources discussed.[7]

Table 5-2 contains an outline of research strategies for North Dakota constitutional issues.

---

7. See Chapter 2 for an overview of basic research techniques; Chapter 4 for a discussion of secondary sources; Chapter 6 for locating annotations in statutory compilations; Chapter 11 for locating annotations accompanying cases; and Chapter 12 for a discussion of Shepard's and KeyCite.

Table 5-2. Outline for Researching North Dakota Constitutional Law Issues

Evaluate what you know so far. Do you already know that your research issue implicates a constitutional provision or are you unsure? Do you have a citation to the constitution or another primary source or are you starting from scratch?

1. **If you already have a citation to the constitution**
   - Check an annotated version of the constitution for citations to statutes, cases, and rules that are implicated by the particular provision.
   - Review the annotations for citations to secondary sources that may analyze your issue in more depth.

2. **If you have a citation to other primary authority**
   - Use the annotations accompanying the statutes, case, or rule that you have found to check for citations to relevant constitutional provisions.

3. **If you are starting from scratch**
   - Browse the online constitution for free at the North Dakota Legislative Branch website.
   - Use the General Index accompanying the *North Dakota Century Code* to identify relevant constitutional provisions and statutes.
   - Consult secondary sources, which will provide an overview of your topic and may lead to citations to North Dakota constitutional provisions.

A. Beginning with a Citation to the Constitution

1. Locating the Text of the Constitution

The text of the North Dakota Constitution is easy to find online in both free and commercial sources. The North Dakota Legislative Branch publishes the constitution for free on its website. To locate it, go to the website and click on the heading for "Constitution."

Both Lexis and Westlaw also publish annotated versions of the constitution. On Lexis, the constitution can most easily be found by using the browsing feature. Narrow first to "Source," then "Jurisdiction," then "North Dakota." From here, scroll down until you find the database "North Dakota Constitution."

On Westlaw, the North Dakota Constitution is published in the same database as state statutes. To locate it, go to "State Materials," then "North Dakota," then "North Dakota Statutes and Court Rules." This will lead you to the table of contents for the database; the state constitution is located near the end of the list.

Finally, an annotated version of the North Dakota Constitution is also published in print in the *North Dakota Century Code* (N.D.C.C.). The N.D.C.C. is the official source for state statutes and will be discussed in further detail later in this chapter and in Chapter 6, Researching North Dakota Statutes.

2. Organization of the North Dakota Constitution

If you already have a citation to the particular provision of the constitution for which you are looking, the North Dakota Constitution is fairly easy to navigate. The constitution is organized first by "article," designated by a roman numeral; each article is then broken into numbered "sections."[8]

For example, if you were provided with the citation N.D. Const. Art. I, §3, you would first navigate to Article I, which is entitled "Declaration of Rights." You would then go to Section 3, where you would find the constitutional provision regarding religious liberty.

3. Using Annotated Versus Unannotated Versions of the Constitution

Like other primary sources of law, the North Dakota Constitution is published in both unannotated and annotated versions. Unannotated versions simply contain the text of the Constitution and nothing more. Annotated versions contain valuable additional information such as citations to state statutes, cases, and rules related to the constitutional provision in question; citations to secondary sources that cite or discuss the particular provision; and historical notes on when the provision was originally adopted or, if applicable, amended.

For this reason, it is virtually always more efficient to use annotated versions of the constitution rather than unannotated versions. The versions of the constitution published on Lexis and Westlaw as well as in the N.D.C.C. are all annotated. The version on the North Dakota State Legislature website is not annotated, but, because it is free, it is a good source to use if you simply need to browse the constitution or read a provision.

B. Beginning with Secondary or Primary Sources

If you are just beginning your research or are unsure whether a state constitutional provision governs or relates to your particular issue, you could begin your research with secondary or primary sources.

---

8. Note that neither the preamble, which is located at the beginning of the constitution, nor the transition schedule, which is located at the end, have article numbers. The transition schedule does have section numbers, but, as of this writing, only Section 26 is in effect. Sections 1-25 have been repealed.

1. Beginning with Secondary Sources

For most types of legal research, the best place to start is with secondary sources. This is not necessarily true in the case of North Dakota constitutional law research because, given the dearth of North Dakota-specific sources, finding references to North Dakota constitutional law in secondary sources is not always easy. While the general secondary sources discussed in Chapter 4 can be quite valuable in obtaining an overview of the law and in locating citations to state statutes, cases, and rules, these sources often do not provide direction citations to the North Dakota Constitution, whether through oversight or because the constitution does not fit in with the structure of the source.

Nonetheless, some secondary sources may prove valuable in researching North Dakota constitutional law. Oxford University Press publishes a series of books on state constitutions, including one called *The North Dakota State Constitution*. This book, published in 2011, provides an historical overview of the state's constitution as well as provision-by-provision commentary. Note, however, that the book is not updated so more recent constitutional amendments are not included.

For a more general overview of state constitutional law, *State Constitutional Law: Litigating Individual Rights, Claims, and Defenses* is a useful treatise published by Michie, a division of LexisNexis. This treatise collects constitutional law cases from all fifty states, comparing and contrasting them both to one another and to federal cases. It provides in-depth analysis of common constitutional issues and includes a table of statutes, a table of cases, and a general index.

Law review articles may be useful if you are able to locate one that thoroughly analyzes your particular research topic. While you may not find an article devoted solely to North Dakota constitutional law, articles geared at analyzing an issue from the perspective of multiple states may prove valuable. Three law journals are devoted exclusively to constitutional law: the *University of Pennsylvania Journal of Constitutional Law*, the *Hastings Constitutional Law Quarterly*, and the *Duke Journal of Constitutional Law and Public Policy*. While these journals cover mostly federal constitutional issues, they do occasionally publish articles geared at state constitutional law. Additionally, both the *Albany Law Review* and the *Rutgers Law Journal* publish annual issues devoted solely to state constitutional law.

Websites may also be of help in identifying and analyzing North Dakota constitutional law issues. For example, the Council of State Governments

(CSG) website for Midwestern states[9] includes a Policy & Research page, divided by topic, that provides policy analysis on a variety of issues facing Midwestern states. The site is searchable, and typing "North Dakota Constitution" into the search box yields a variety of articles on constitutional issues in North Dakota. The CSG also publishes the *Book of the States*, a yearly reference book that covers, among other topics, trends and updates in state constitutional law. The book has been published since 1935 and is available for free on the CSG website: click on the link for "CSG Knowledge Center" and then "Publications."

Because of the limitations of secondary sources when researching North Dakota constitutional issues, the best strategy is still to use the secondary sources to first locate citations to primary authority, such as statutes, cases, or rules. Then use sources publishing those authorities to identify relevant constitutional provisions, as described in the following section.

2. Beginning with Primary Sources

In the course of your research, you will identify relevant primary authority, such as statutes, cases, or rules. These primary authorities are published in a variety of sources, but annotated versions will provide you with citations to any North Dakota constitutional provisions implicated by the primary authority in question.

If you do not already have a citation to other primary authority, you should first use the research techniques appropriate to those various sources to locate relevant primary authority. Because those techniques are described in detail in other chapters, they will not be repeated here.

One particular primary source is worth noting, however. Because the North Dakota Constitution is published in the *North Dakota Century Code*, it can be accessed via the N.D.C.C. index, which is published in both the print version and on Westlaw. Using this index can therefore allow you to kill two birds with one stone, researching both statutes that may lead you to constitutional provisions and the constitution itself.

For example, if you were researching freedom of religion in North Dakota, you could go to the N.D.C.C. index and look up "Religion." Here, you would find many subheadings leading not only to relevant statutes but to constitutional provisions as well. There is even a subheading called "Constitution of North Dakota," that identifies multiple sub-subheadings for which there are related constitutional provisions, including one specifically entitled "Freedom of Religion."

---

9. *See* http://www.csgmidwest.org.

IV. Researching Proposed Amendments

You may, in some instances, need to consult either current or historical proposed constitutional amendments. For example, you may need to look at current proposed constitutional amendments to keep abreast of possible upcoming changes in your area of research. Constitutional amendments currently under consideration can be found at the North Dakota Legislative Branch website. First, click on the current legislative session. Then, use the "Major Topic Index to Bills," to find the category "Constitutional Amendments." This will lead you to the full text of proposed amendments as well as information on any legislative action that has been taken thus far.

You are less likely to need *historical amendments*—amendments that were proposed, voted on, and defeated, in the past—in ordinary practice, but they may be of interest in compiling a legislative history[10] or tracking legal developments and community attitudes over time.

Past proposed constitutional amendments, including those that were not adopted, can be found with the North Dakota session laws, published biannually as the *Laws of North Dakota*. Along with many other materials,[11] this publication includes the text of proposed amendments and designates which amendments passed and which did not.

The best way to find past proposed constitutional amendments is to first browse the full list of past amendments on the North Dakota Legislative Branch website. This list can be found under the "Research Center" link. From there, click on "Measures Before The Voters." This link will take you to an up-to-date chronological list of amendments[12] that have been proposed since 1889. The list provides a brief description of each amendment, the method of proposal (for example, by legislative referral or by initiative), the vote tally for and against, whether the amendment was accepted or rejected by voters (designated by an "A" or an "R"), and the page number in *Laws of North Dakota* where the text of the amendment is located.

However, the "Measures Before The Voters" document includes only a brief description of each amendment. To access the full text, you must consult the session laws. Session laws back to the 1985-86 legislative session can be found

---

10. For more information on compiling legislative histories, see Chapter 7.

11. For more information on the types of materials included in *Laws of North Dakota*, see Chapter 6 discussing statutory research.

12. This list also includes other initiatives and referenda, which are discussed in more detail in Chapter 13, Ballot Measures.

on the North Dakota Legislative Branch website, but finding proposed and rejected constitutional amendments on that site is not intuitive. Here's how to do it: First, navigate to the legislative session in question. Next, click on the link for the session laws, and find the section for "chapter categories," which is organized by topic. Most of the topics are organized alphabetically; however, the headings for "Constitutional Amendments Proposed," "Constitutional Amendments Approved," and "Constitutional Amendments Disapproved," are included near the end of the list. You can also check the "General Index" for the heading "Constitutional Amendments."

To access the full text of older proposed constitutional amendments, you will need to go directly to the appropriate volume (organized by legislative session) of *Laws of North Dakota*. This publication is available on HeinOnline back to 1889.[13] This publication is also available in print. With these sources, you can use the page number gleaned from the "Measures Before The Voters" list to find the amendment or consult the "General Index" under the heading "Constitutional Amendments."

V. State Constitutional Interpretation

Volumes have been written about the appropriate methods to interpret federal constitutional provisions; much less analysis has been devoted to how to interpret state constitutions. This lack of guidance on state constitutional interpretation raises some interesting questions. For example, when a legal issue arises that implicates both the state and federal constitution, which should be analyzed first? Some scholars argue that the federal constitution should always be interpreted first, and courts should resort to the state constitution only if the issue is not fully settled under federal law. Others argue the opposite—that the state constitution should be considered first and the federal constitution considered only if there is a clear pre-emption question or the parties raise the issue.

Another question that may arise is how to read a state constitutional provision that is similar, but not identical to, a federal constitutional provision.

---

13. Although North Dakota session laws are also available on Lexis and Westlaw, the coverage in these services does not go back as far as those available for free on the North Dakota Legislative Assembly website. Additionally, neither of these paid services provides a clear method for accessing the portion of the session laws dedicated to constitutional amendments; therefore, these services are not recommended for finding past proposed amendments.

Should state courts interpret the state provision the same way the federal courts have interpreted the federal provision? Or should they analyze the differences in the provisions, even if they are slight, and develop a separate, state-specific interpretation?

These questions have no clear, definitive answers, so you must be aware of the methods of interpretation favored by each state. In North Dakota, the state Supreme Court has said that "[w]hen interpreting the state constitution, our overriding objective is to give effect to the intent and purpose of the people adopting the constitutional statement."[14] The Court looks first to the text of the provision, giving it "its plain, ordinary, and commonly understood meaning."[15] The Court will also look to reconcile any conflicts between provisions and has stated, "We presume the people do not intend absurd or ludicrous results in adopting constitutional provisions, and we therefore construe such provisions to avoid those results."[16]

Beyond textual interpretation, the Court may also consult the legislative history of a provision or even the political climate that existed when the provision was adopted.[17] The political climate takes on special significance in states like North Dakota that submit all amendments for popular vote and allow voters to propose amendments through the initiative process.

Finally, keep in mind that, in North Dakota, four out of the five justices on the state Supreme Court must concur in order to find a law unconstitutional. This requirement for a super-majority contrasts with the practice on the U.S. Supreme Court and on most other appellate courts, which require only a bare majority to hold a law unconstitutional.

---

14. *City of Bismarck v. Fettig*, 601 N.W.2d 247, 250 (N.D. 1999).

15. *Tormaschy v. Hjell*, 210 N.W.2d 100, 102 (N.D. 1973).

16. *North Dakota Comm'n on Med. Competency v. Racek*, 527 N.W.2d 262, 266 (N.D. 1995).

17. For further details on compiling a legislative history, see Chapter 7, Legislative History.

Chapter 6

Statutes

I. Introduction

When most people think about "the law," statutes are what probably come to mind. Statutes are the laws enacted by legislative bodies, like Congress. They may govern a wide array of matters from prohibitions against employment discrimination to the proper containment of farm animals. While not every legal issue will be governed by statute, if a statute exists, it will take precedence over other types of laws like cases and administrative regulations. Therefore, when researching a new legal issue, you should always check to see if there is an applicable statute. This chapter will show you how to research statutes and how to analyze them.

II. Lawmaking in North Dakota

The legislative body in North Dakota is called the Legislative Assembly. Like the United States Congress, it is made up of two houses: the Senate and the House of Representatives. The Legislative Assembly meets biennially (every other year), convening in January of odd-numbered years, and the legislative session lasts for eighty days. In addition to its regular meetings, the legislature occasionally has special sessions if a pressing matter arises between ordinary sessions. For example, on March 20–28, 1944, during the heart of World War II, then-Governor John Moses convened a special session to draft absentee voting legislation for those in the military.

A. *Laws of North Dakota*

When the Legislative Assembly first enacts a law, it is published as a *session law* in a volume called the *Laws of North Dakota*. The *Laws of North Dakota* is published after each legislative session, including special sessions. In addition to newly passed laws, the *Laws of North Dakota* also includes the Governor's veto messages, resolutions,[1] and measures that have been submitted to the electorate between sessions.

Session laws in the *Laws of North Dakota* are organized chronologically. As a result, you cannot research laws by topic in *Laws of North Dakota*. Nevertheless, the publication may be useful in researching some of the supplemental materials mentioned above, like resolutions and veto messages, that are not included in the statutory code. *Laws of North Dakota* may also be useful if you want to examine laws passed during particular legislative sessions.

B. *North Dakota Century Code*

In addition to being published as session laws, statutes are *codified*, meaning they are organized by topic. The best place to research statutes is in North Dakota's official code, the *North Dakota Century Code* (N.D.C.C.).[2] The N.D.C.C. is divided by subject into numbered "titles." At first glance, there appear to be sixty-five numbered titles. However, there are actually seventy-two in total because seven of the titles provide separate designations for specific sub-topics within the title's overarching topic. For example, Title 15 covers Education, and Title 15.1 covers Elementary and Secondary Education. Table 6-1 shows all of the titles in the N.D.C.C.

The titles are sub-divided into chapters, and the chapters are further sub-divided into sections. While each section technically represents an individual statute, you will often need to read the surrounding sections, too, to get a full picture of the law. For example, Title 34, Chapter 7 covers Child Labor and is divided into twenty-one sections. Section 1 prohibits the employment of minors under fourteen, and Section 6 covers the type of evidence that may be submitted to prove the age of a minor.

Citation references to individual laws will include all three of these elements: title, chapter, and section number. A citation to the "Evidence of age of minor" statute in the official code might look like this: N.D.C.C. § 34-07-

---

1. Resolutions are not laws. They are formal expressions of a legislative body's opinions. They are typically used to show support for a particular cause, regardless of whether there is currently a law in place addressing that issue. For example, since the Supreme Court's opinion in *Citizens United v. FEC*, 558 U.S. 310 (2010), several states have passed resolutions related to campaign finance reform.

Table 6-1. Titles in the *North Dakota Century Code*

1. General Provisions	22. Guaranty, Indemnity, and Suretyship	45. Partnerships
2. Areonautics	23. Health and Safety	46. Printing Laws
3. Agency	24. Highways, Bridges, and Ferries	47. Property
4. Agriculture	25. Mental and Physical Illness or Disability	48. Public Buildings
4.1 Agriculture	26. Insurance	49. Public Utilities
5. Alcoholic Beverages	26.1 Insurance	50. Public Welfare
6. Banks and Banking	27. Judicial Branch of Government	51. Sales and Exchanges
7. Building and Loan Associations	28. Judicial Branch, Civil	52. Social Security
8. Carriage	29. Judicial Branch, Criminal	53. Sports and Amusements
9. Contracts and Obligations	30. Judicial Procedure, Probate	54. State Government
10. Corporations	30.1 Uniform Probate Code	55. State Historical Society and State Parks
11. Counties	31. Judicial Proof	56. Succession and Wills
12. Corrections, Parole, and Probation	32. Judicial Remedies	57. Taxation
12.1 Criminal Code	33. County Justice Court	58. Townships
13. Debtor and Creditor Relationship	34. Labor and Employment	59. Trusts
14. Domestic Relations and Persons	35. Liens	60. Warehousing and Deposits
15. Education	36. Livestock	61. Waters
15.1 Elementary and Secondary Education	37. Military	62. Weapons
16. Elections	38. Mining and Gas and Oil Production	62.1. Weapons

Table 6-1. Titles in the *North Dakota Century Code, continued*

16.1 Elections	39. Motor Vehicles	63. Weeds
17. Energy	40. Municipal Government	
18. Fires	41. Uniform Commercial Code	
19. Foods, Drugs, Oils, and Compounds	42. Nuisances	
20. Game, Fish, and Predators	43. Occupations and Professions	
20.1 Game, Fish, Predators, and Boating	44. Offices and Officers	

06.[2] This citation indicates that the law can be found in Title 34, Chapter 7, Section 6.

III. Researching North Dakota Statutes

When you already have a citation to a statute, the process for finding the statute is fairly straightforward. In print research, simply locate the correct volume by looking at the title numbers on the spines of the books, then flip to the appropriate chapter. Online, you can either use the table of contents to locate the appropriate title or, if available, use a search function to find the statute by citation.[3]

However, more often than not, you will be presented with either (1) a legal issue where you either know that a statute exists, but you don't know where to find it, or (2) you are not sure if a statute exists at all, and you need to find out.

One way of finding out whether there is a statute governing a given topic is to begin your research in secondary sources (covered in Chapter 4, Secondary Sources). While this is often the best method to use for federal statutes and in

---

2. Note that this citation format is a modification used in North Dakota state courts. The official format for citing to North Dakota state statutes is N.D. Cent. Code § 34-07-06.

3. More information on how and where to find citations online is provided in Part III.B.

many states, you may find secondary sources somewhat less helpful in North Dakota. While some secondary sources will certainly mention North Dakota statutes, there are virtually no North Dakota-specific secondary sources. So, you will typically need to supplement your research by researching directly in the statutes themselves. Additionally, even if you do find a statute referenced in a secondary source, you should always double-check the statutes themselves to ensure that you didn't miss anything.

North Dakota statutes can be researched both in print and online. Typically, statutes are easiest to work with in print because the books allow you the ability to easily flip back and forth to see the immediately preceding and succeeding sections. However, due to North Dakota's large geographical size and sparse, widely dispersed population, print codes may be unavailable in many areas. Therefore, practically speaking, you may find yourself conducting statutory research online more often than in print. Regardless of which method you use, the general process, as summarized in Figure 6-1, is largely the same. The next two sections describe how to find statutes both in print and online, noting any differences between the methods.

A. Researching North Dakota Statutes in Print

The N.D.C.C. in print contains all of the state's statutes and court rules, extensive research annotations, and a comprehensive index. While some states publish their own official codes, the N.D.C.C. is published by a commercial publisher, Michie, a division of LexisNexis.[4] This is important because, unlike most state publishers, commercial publishers like Matthew Bender typically include annotations that lead the researcher to other sources that have interpreted the statute. The N.D.C.C.'s annotations include references to cases, law reviews, and A.L.R.s.

Although the North Dakota Legislative Assembly meets biennially, it would not be cost-effective to publish an entire new set of the code every two years. Instead, the statutes are updated with *pocket parts* after each legislative session. Pocket parts are soft-bound inserts placed in the back of each volume containing annotated statutes that have been enacted since the last time the volume was

---

4. The official print version of the N.D.C.C. is technically entitled the *North Dakota Century Code Annotated*. However, this longer name is virtually never used in the state. It has been shortened here both to reflect common usage and to avoid confusion with the unofficial print version, *West's North Dakota Century Code Annotated*.

Figure 6-1. Researching Statutes

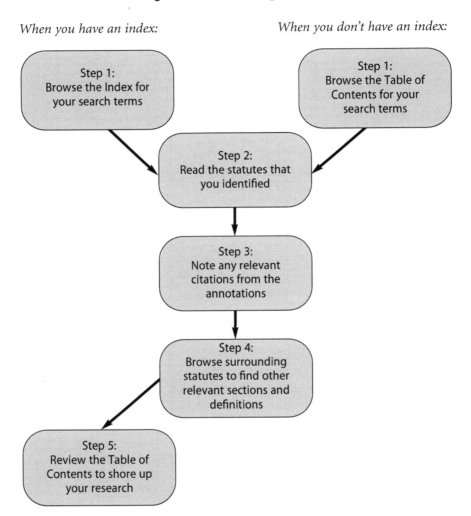

When you have an index: *When you don't have an index:*

published. The pocket parts allow you to ensure that your research is relatively up-to-date. New volumes are not printed until the pocket parts become so large that they are unwieldy.

Assuming you are unable to locate a statute via a secondary source, the first step in researching statutes is to consult your list of search terms, which you generated in Chapter 1. Remember to review your list of terms to determine whether you need to refine or expand them. Imagine you have been asked to research the child labor laws referenced in Part II.B of this chapter. You might generate these terms: children, work, underage, employment, etc.

Next, consult the index. A comprehensive, alphabetical index to the statutes is included at the end of the entire set of volumes. The index will guide you to the appropriate statutory section or sections in the volumes. Some index terms may lead you directly to a given statute; others might instead direct you to other terms in the index. You should look up those terms as well. Figure 6-2 shows the page in the index where the phrase "child labor" is located.

The index will not provide you with specific page numbers; instead, you will see a title, chapter, and section number, like 34-07-01. You can easily locate the given section because the title numbers are printed on the spines of the volumes. Once you have the correct volume, simply flip through to the appropriate section. Note that each volume also includes a table of contents. You should consult this tool as well because it will allow you to quickly see what is covered in the surrounding statutory sections. This context will give you a big picture view of the area of law you're researching.

Once you find your statute, read it carefully and jot down any pertinent citations from the annotations. Then, check the pocket part in the back of the volume to ensure that there have not been any changes to your statute since the last time the volume was published. One note of caution: if the pocket part indicates that the statute has changed since the last time the volume was published, make sure to look at the date on which it was amended. While the current version of the statute is the version that typically governs, under certain circumstances, the older statute may still be governing law. An example of one of those circumstances is when someone was accused of committing a crime before a statute was amended but was charged and prosecuted after it was amended.

B. Researching North Dakota Statutes Online

The N.D.C.C. is readily available online in multiple sources. This section covers a few of those online sources in detail and briefly mentions a few other online resources as well.

1. Finding Statutes on Westlaw and Lexis

The N.D.C.C. is available on both Westlaw and Lexis, although coverage varies somewhat. The database on Westlaw contains current annotated North Dakota statutes, court rules, and the state constitution. There is an unannotated version of the current code as well as more specific databases for particular laws, such as "North Dakota Blue Sky Statutes." Additionally, older versions of

Figure 6-2. Sample Index Page

108 INDEX

Source: *North Dakota Century Code* Index. Reprinted with permission from LexisNexis.

the statutes are available back to 2008. Lexis contains the current annotated statutes, court rules, and constitution. Older versions of the code are available back to 1991.

Westlaw also includes the statutes index. The statutes index is organized alphabetically by subject and is searchable by keyword. Additionally, both Westlaw and Lexis include the table of contents for the statutes. On both services, the table of contents is organized by title. Either one of these places—the index or the table of contents—is a good place to start when trying to identify a statute by topic.

Westlaw also provides a Popular Name Table. The Popular Name Table makes it easy to find statutes that are typically referred to by name rather than by citation, such as the "Abortion Control Act."

You can also search both Westlaw and Lexis using a terms and connectors search or a natural language search. This full-text search, however, is generally not the preferred method of searching statutes. Statutes often contain specific, complicated language, and it may be difficult and time consuming to brainstorm correct search terms. However, if you have an idea of the specific language of a statute, terms and connectors searching may be helpful.

2. The Benefits of Using Westlaw and Lexis

The benefit of searching in Westlaw or Lexis rather than on the free government sites discussed in the next section is that these commercial services include annotations that are similar to those provided in the print version. The annotations include citations to legislative history documents and secondary sources. Most helpful, Westlaw includes "Notes of Decisions" and Lexis includes "Case Notes." Both features provide brief descriptions of cases that have applied or interpreted the particular statute. Both Westlaw and Lexis provide hyperlinks to annotated sources, making it easy to access those sources.

Westlaw and Lexis also have an advantage over the print version because they are updated more quickly. Both Westlaw and Lexis include small "i" icons next to database names, which take you to a page describing the content of the database and how regularly it is updated. For some databases on Westlaw, this page also provides citation information, search tips, and links to related databases.

3. North Dakota Legislative Branch

As a free public service, the North Dakota Legislative Branch's website includes the complete North Dakota Century Code.[5] The code can be found by clicking on the "Century Code" link under the "Laws and Constitution" heading. All of the titles appear as links on one page, making it easy to browse by topic. Clicking on a link brings up links to the individual chapters, and clicking on a chapter link will then bring up the statutes, organized by section number. Another approach is to enter a search term in the "Search" box at the top right of the screen.

The chief advantages to researching the code on the Legislative Branch's website are that it is free and well organized. A major disadvantage is that it does not include the annotations available in the print codes and in commercial databases.

4. Other Online Databases

Many other commercial online services provide state statutes, including Casemaker, Fastcase, VersusLaw, Loislaw, and Bloomberg Law. These databases tend to be less expensive than Westlaw and Lexis, and Casemaker is free for North Dakota law students and members of the North Dakota bar. Although these services each have their own unique searching capabilities and coverage, you can use the basic searching techniques covered in the discussion of Westlaw and Lexis.

C. Historical Versions of the Official Code

On very rare occasions, you may need to look at older versions of the North Dakota code. This might happen if, for example, you were asked to trace the evolution of a law that was enacted many years ago and has since been amended or repealed. While it is exceedingly unlikely that you would be asked to do this in ordinary day-to-day practice, it is worthwhile to know about older versions of the code.

The North Dakota code was named the *North Dakota Century Code* in 1959 in honor of the 100th anniversary of North Dakota's designation as a U.S. territory, which happened in 1861. As a result, it does not appear as the official title until the 1959–60 publication year. Prior codes include *The Revised Codes of North Dakota 1895*, *The Revised Codes of North Dakota 1899*, *The Revised*

---

5. The North Dakota Legislative Branch's website is www.legis.nd.gov.

Codes of North Dakota 1905, *The Compiled Laws of North Dakota 1913*, *The Compiled Laws of North Dakota 1913–1925*, and *The North Dakota Revised Code of 1943*.

In 1947, the state legislature authorized the Secretary of State to publish single-volume supplements to the 1943 code in order to update it with laws that were passed after the code's publication. These supplements were published in 1947, 1949, 1953, and 1957. Permanent supplements are no longer published; instead, as discussed in Part III.A. of this chapter, the print version of the N.D.C.C. is updated with pocket parts after each legislative session.

IV. Applying and Interpreting State Statutes

Simply finding a statute is not enough. You also need to know how to interpret and apply the statute. Interpreting and applying statutes involves a multi-step process.

First, find and read the statute. To interpret it, you must then figure out what it means. It is rare for a statute to be clear and complete by itself. Instead, several sections will work together, and statutory language can sometimes be ambiguous. To interpret the statute, you should browse the statutes that come just before and after your statute in the code to help you understand the language. These statutes will typically be on related matters and may or may not be helpful. Additionally, you should look for any nearby statutes that might define the terms in your statute. Legislatures often, but not always, include sections with definitions of important terms.

Next, you should research cases that have interpreted the relevant provision of the statute. Recall that both the print code and databases available on Westlaw and Lexis include annotations that can help you locate relevant cases.

Additionally, you should try to interpret the statute through the eyes of a judge. In interpreting statutes, judges will first look at the plain language of the statute. In other words, they will ask themselves what the statute means on its face. They will also look to other sources, including prior case interpretations, to assist them in understanding how the law applies. Finally, they may also look at its legislative history to understand the purpose of the statute. The legislative history includes amendments that were proposed and rejected, records of debates in the legislature, and hearings that were held on the statute. Researching North Dakota legislative history is covered in Chapter 7.

Chapter 7

Legislative History and Bill Tracking

I. Introduction

Chapter 6 explained how to research and interpret statutes. Every statute has a history that can affect a court's interpretation. Statutes begin as "bills," and each bill that is ultimately enacted typically goes through multiple iterations. As the bill passes through the various stages of the legislative process on its way to becoming a law, legislative committees and individuals create documents. Legislative history research involves collecting and analyzing those documents.

Legislative history documents are not technically law. Because legislative history documents are created prior to the enactment of a statute, they are not part of the official code and are not binding on the courts or other state actors. So why should you bother researching legislative history?

The chief use of legislative history is as a statutory interpretation tool; in other words, the documents created prior to a bill becoming a law can assist the courts in determining what that law means. Under North Dakota law, statutes are to be interpreted based on their plain meaning;[1] however, if the statutory language is ambiguous, the statute may be interpreted by the use of certain other materials, including legislative history.[2] Legislative history documents may be valuable because they often include the legislators' own views on what the bill means and why various changes are made to it as it makes its way through the legislative process.

Related, but not identical, to legislative history research is bill tracking. Bill tracking involves exactly what it sounds like — tracking a new bill as it makes its way through the legislative process. Bill tracking is useful for anticipating upcoming changes in the law. Both legislative history research and bill tracking are the focus of this chapter.

---

1. N.D. Cent. Code § 1-02-05 (2009).
2. N.D. Cent. Code § 1-02-39 (2009).

II. How a Bill Becomes a Law in North Dakota

Crucial to effectively conducting legislative history research or tracking a bill is understanding how a bill becomes a law in North Dakota. Once you understand the legislative process, you will be better able to understand what kinds of documents are produced and, most importantly, how to find them.

A. Legislative Management

As discussed in Chapter 6, Statutes, the Legislative Assembly meets biennially (every other year), convening in January of odd-numbered years. The legislative session lasts for eighty days; however, much work is also being done between sessions. This work is led by a body called the Legislative Management.[3]

The Legislative Management is composed of seventeen legislators, appointed after each legislative session, as well as a large staff of attorneys, researchers, accountants, and other personnel known as the Legislative Council. Between sessions, members of the Legislative Management serve on a variety of interim committees, some of which have been designated by statute and others of which are established by the Legislative Management.

The work of the Legislative Management and the Legislative Council includes, but is not limited to, conducting studies, holding hearings, and taking testimony from interested parties. The purpose is, in essence, to determine the agenda for the next legislative session.

In November, before the start of a legislative session, the Legislative Management meets to discuss all committee work and votes to accept, reject, or amend committee reports. The Legislative Management then presents its recommendations, including drafts of implementing bills and resolutions, to the Legislative Assembly for consideration.

B. The Legislative Process

The North Dakota Legislative Assembly comprises a Senate and a House of Representatives. Bills may be introduced in either the Senate or the House, but the process of enacting bills in each is similar.

---

3. From its inception in 1945 until 1969, the Legislative Management was known as the Legislative Research Committee. From 1969 to 2009, the Legislative Management was known as the Legislative Council. Note that there is still a body known as the Legislative Council; this name now refers to selected staff members who work for the Legislative Management.

First, the bill is introduced by a legislator, assigned a number,[4] and read to other legislators (the "first reading"). The bill is then assigned to a committee; in the Senate, this assignment is made by the Lieutenant Governor and, in the House, this assignment is made by the Speaker of the House.

The committee discusses the bill and holds a public hearing before making a final report and recommendation to the rest of the Senate or House, depending on where the bill was introduced. The committee may report the bill with or without amendment and either favorably, unfavorably, or without any recommendation. The committee also has the option of requesting that the bill be referred to another committee with or without amendment.

After the committee reports, the bill[5] is put on the calendar. On the date indicated, the bill is read again (the "second reading"). The bill is then debated on the floor of the chamber in which it was introduced, and a vote is taken. If the bill passes, it is referred to the other chamber.

The other chamber then repeats the procedure. If the bill is passed in the same form, it is "enrolled" and sent to the Governor. If it is passed with an amendment, it must be sent back to the other chamber for reconsideration. Only after the bill has been passed in the same form by both the Senate and House will it be enrolled and presented to the Governor. In some instances, a conference committee consisting of both Senators and Representatives may be convened to make recommendations to both chambers to ensure the passage of the bill in the same form in each.

Once the bill is presented to the Governor, it becomes law if the Governor either signs it or forwards it to the Secretary of State without signature. If the Governor vetoes the bill, it may still become law if the veto is overridden by a two-thirds vote in both the Senate and the House.

Once enacted bills are on file with the Secretary of State, most go into effect the following August 1. Tax and appropriations bills typically go into effect on July 1.

Table 7-1 summarizes the legislative process in North Dakota and indicates the types of documents that are created at each stage in the process.

---

4. The first bill of the session in the House will be number 1001; in the Senate, the first bill is 2001.

5. If an amendment was proposed, the amendment will be placed on the calendar first. Only after the amendment is accepted or rejected will the bill be placed on the calendar.

Table 7-1. Summary of the Legislative Process in North Dakota and Accompanying Documents

Stage in the Process	Accompanying Documents
Legislative Management committees meet, conduct studies, hold hearings, and perform other work in preparation for the upcoming legislative session.	Background memoranda; committee meeting minutes, including hearing testimony; reports
Bill is introduced in the House or Senate	Original version of bill
Bill is assigned to a committee, which holds a public hearing and deliberates. The committee may suggest amendments at this time, which will be submitted to the full chamber in which the bill was introduced.	Committee meeting minutes, including hearing testimony; possible amendments/different versions of the bill
Committee reports the bill, with its recommendation, to the full chamber in which it was introduced; a vote is taken.	Bill report; final version of bill voted on; vote tally
If the bill passes, it goes to the other chamber and the above process is repeated, beginning with the introduction of the bill. If there are discrepancies between the versions of the bill passed in each chamber, a conference committee may be called to resolve the differences. The bill must be approved by both the House and Senate before being sent to the Governor.	Conference committee (if any) report
Bill is presented to the Governor for signature.	Enrolled bill
Governor takes action: signs the bill, presents it to the Secretary of State without signature, or vetoes it.	Signing statement (if any) or veto message (if any)

III. Legislative History

Legislative history research can be quite time consuming and complex, depending on the age of the statute in question. For newer laws, much information is now available and easily accessible online; however, for older laws, documents will typically be available only in print. Keep in mind that, given the difficulty of locating some documents as well as the fact that such documents are not technically law, you may reach a point in your research in which the costs in time and energy of finding every single document outweigh the benefits. Therefore, when you're working under a time crunch, it may be best to prioritize some legislative history documents over others. As a general rule, the more that legislators are involved in the creation of a document, the more valuable the document is. So, for example, a committee report would carry more weight than record of testimony from a member of the public.

A. Sources of Legislative History

Table 7-1 noted the documents that are produced at each stage of the legislative process, including those produced by the Legislative Management. This section of the chapter explains those documents in more detail. Part III.B will describe how to research and retrieve documents.

1. Legislative Management Documents

Recall that, between sessions of the Legislative Assembly, the Legislative Management does a significant amount of work and essentially creates the agenda for the upcoming legislative session. The Legislative Management is composed of many committees, corresponding roughly with the ordinary Legislative Assembly committees as well as the Legislative Council, which provides research and guidance. Documents created during this interim session may assist you in determining the original purpose of a bill as well as provide background information as to why it was drafted as it was.

a. Background Memoranda

Legislative Management background memoranda are prepared by the Legislative Council to assist interim committees in their work. The content of such memoranda varies, but their purpose is to assist the committee in understanding the main issue or issues before it. They may include information such as statistics, public testimony, and recommendations.

b. Legislative Management Committee Meeting Minutes

The Legislative Management Committees, in addition to their own deliberations, also hold hearings on the matters before them. Committee meeting minutes include information presented to the committee by the Legislative Council staff as well as written testimony from third parties. The minutes may also include drafts of suggested bills and resolutions for presentation to the entire Legislative Management.

c. Legislative Management Reports

In the November prior to each biennial legislative session, reports from the interim committees are presented to the full Legislative Management for acceptance, amendment, or rejection. The Legislative Management then submits a report to the Governor and the Legislative Assembly containing summaries of interim committee reports, a discussion of committee findings, and recommendations that were accepted by the full Legislative Management. The report also includes summaries of bills and resolutions required to implement the recommendations. For some recommendations, the report also includes a discussion of laws that will be affected by the recommendations or a summary of the testimony and other information received by the interim committee. Some reports include both a discussion and a summary.

2. Legislative Assembly Documents

a. Versions of Bills

Versions of bills are a major source in legislative history research. Most bills go through multiple incarnations before eventual passage. By examining bills as originally proposed and the amendments to those bills that were passed or rejected before final passage, you may be able to better understand how the statute that resulted from the bill should be read. For example, if you want to argue for a particular interpretation of a word or phrase in a bill, it would be helpful to know what other words or phrases, if any, had been considered. If a word with an alternate meaning from the one you believe to be correct had actually been considered and rejected, that could strengthen your argument.

b. Committee Hearings

All proposed bills undergo a public hearing before the legislative committee in charge of the bill. Testimony is accepted from any interested member of the public. These hearings are transcribed and published.

c. Committee Minutes and Reports (Including Conference Committees)

Each committee keeps minutes of its meetings. Like hearings, these minutes are transcribed and published. Committees also make final reports to the legislature as a whole, which are transcribed with the minutes. Reports may briefly explain the purpose of the bill in question and any changes that were made. Additionally, reports include the committee's recommendation on the bill, such as whether it should be passed, not passed, or amended. If a conference committee was convened to resolve differences between the House and Senate versions of the bills, there will also be minutes and a report for that committee.

d. Floor Debates

Floor debates are the debates of House or Senate members regarding a particular bill. Floor debates are not routinely published; instead, a legislator may request to have his or her remarks published.

e. Attorney General Opinions

Attorney General opinions are written opinions issued by the Attorney General in response to legal questions posed by public officials, administrative agencies, and state and local officials. Although researching Attorney General opinions is discussed in Chapter 8, Administrative Law, they are mentioned briefly here because some Attorney General opinions are issued in response to legislators' requests for a legal opinion on a given bill.

f. Governor's Statements

Before a bill becomes a law, it must be signed by the Governor or sent to the Secretary of State without signature. On occasion, the Governor will include a statement with his or her signature, called a *signing statement*. This statement typically explains why the Governor has signed the bill and may describe his or her understanding of what it means.

Additionally, the Governor has the option of vetoing the bill. As with signing statements, when the Governor vetoes a bill, he or she may include a *veto message* explaining the reason for the action taken.

B. Finding the Documents

1. Locating the Bill Number

The key to finding legislative history documents is to first find the bill number for the statute in question. Finding the bill number is a two step process.

First, you must locate the statute in an annotated version of the North Dakota Century Code (N.D.C.C.). The print version of the N.D.C.C. is annotated as are the versions available on Lexis and Westlaw.[6]

Once you have located the statute in an annotated code, look for the "History" (or, on Westlaw, "Credits") information found at the end of the statute.

---

6. For a reminder of how to access the N.D.C.C., see Chapter 6, Statutes.

Figure 7-1. North Dakota Harassment Statute on Lexis

12.1-17-07. Harassment.

1. A person is guilty of an offense if, with intent to frighten or harass another, the person:

   a. Communicates in writing or by electronic communication a threat to inflict injury on any person, to any person's reputation, or to any property;

   b. Makes a telephone call anonymously or in offensively coarse language;

   c. Makes repeated telephone calls or other electronic communication, whether or not a conversation ensues, with no purpose of legitimate communication; or

   d. Communicates a falsehood in writing or by electronic communication and causes mental anguish.

2. The offense is a class A misdemeanor if it is under subdivision a of subsection 1 or subsection 4. Otherwise it is a class B misdemeanor.

3. Any offense defined herein and committed by use of electronic communication may be deemed to have been committed at either the place at which the electronic communication was made or at the place where the electronic communication was received.

4. A person is guilty of an offense if the person initiates communication with a 911 emergency line, public safety answering point, or an emergency responder communication system with the intent to annoy or harass another person or a public safety agency or who makes a false report to a public safety agency.

   a. Intent to annoy or harass is established by proof of one or more calls with no legitimate emergency purpose.

   b. Upon conviction of a violation of this subsection, a person is also liable for all costs incurred by any unnecessary emergency response.

5. Any offense defined herein is deemed communicated in writing if it is transmitted electronically, by electronic mail, facsimile, or other similar means. Electronic communication means transfer of signs, signals, writing, images, sounds, data, or intelligence of any nature transmitted in whole or in part by a wire, radio, electromagnetic, photo-electronic, or photo-optical system.

History

S.L. 1973, ch. 116, § 17; 1975, ch. 116, § 16; 1995, ch. 125, § 1; 1999, ch. 124, § 1; 2013, ch. 103, § 1.

Source: Lexis Advance. Reprinted with permission from Reed Elsevier.

This section provides citations to the session laws. Recall from Chapter 6, Part II.A that when a bill is first passed in North Dakota it is published as a *session law* in a publication called *Laws of North Dakota*.[7] The citations in the "History" or "Credits" section of the annotated code refer to this publication. If more than one citation is listed, the first citation is to the version of the statute as it was originally passed; later citations are to the session laws for subsequent amendments to the statute.

Figure 7-1 shows the Lexis page for N.D.C.C. 12.1-17-07, the North Dakota statute defining the crime of harassment.

Notice the information provided in the "History" section at the bottom of the page. The first citation, S.L. 1973, ch. 116, § 17, is the citation for the version of the bill as it was originally passed. The information tells you that version can be found in the 1973 volume of the session laws, in Section 17

---

7. Note that, in spite of the session laws publication having this official name, this title is rarely used. Instead, items in this publication are typically referred to as simply appearing in the "session laws."

of chapter 116. The subsequent citations, although they do not repeat the "S.L.," are also to the session laws. For example, the last citation in the list, 2013, ch. 103, § 1, tells you that this statute was amended in 2013 and that you can find that amendment in the 2013 version of the session laws, at Section 1 of Chapter 103.

Obtaining the session law citation is only the first step in finding the bill number. Next, you need to go to the session laws themselves. The session laws are available in print and online. The North Dakota Legislative Branch website[8] includes session laws back to 1985; HeinOnline provides them back to 1889. Some coverage of North Dakota sessions laws is also available on Lexis and Westlaw; if the particular session law that you are looking for is available on one of those services, then it will show up as a link in the "History" or "Credits" section.

For the harassment statute referenced in Figure 7-1, imagine you wanted to find the bill number for the 2013 amendment. Lexis provides a link to the session law for this amendment, so you can simply click on that link. Figure 7-2 shows a screen shot of the page from the session laws that appears when clicking on that link.

Note that the bill number appears at the top of the page. Here, the bill number for the 2013 amendment to the harassment statute is listed as 2013 N.D. HB 1320: this bill was passed in North Dakota in 2013, which, of course, you already knew. The relevant portion, then, is the citation HB 1320. The "HB" shows that this bill originated in the House of Representatives; a Senate bill would be prefaced "SB." 1320 is the number of this particular bill.

Because coverage on Lexis and Westlaw is limited, and because you may not always be working with the annotated code on one of those services, you must know how to access this bill from the North Dakota Legislative Branch website. From the home page, scroll to the bottom and click on the link for "Session Laws," then choose "2013 Session Laws." Next, click on "Chapter Categories." This section lists the chapter categories by name in alphabetical order, with the chapter number in parentheses next to the category in question. You know from the session law citation that the session law you are looking for was in Chapter 103, so scroll through the list of chapter categories until you find the Criminal Code, which covers Chapters 102-114. See Figure 7-3 for a screen shot of this page. Note the entry "Criminal Code (Chapters 102-114)" on the left.

---

8. *See* http://www.legis.nd.gov.

Figure 7-2. Session Law Excerpt on Lexis

2013 N.D. HB 1320

Copy Citation

Enacted, April 12, 2013

Reporter

2013 N.D. ALS 103 | 2013 N.D. Laws 103 | 2013 N.D. Ch. 103 | 2013 N.D. HB 1320

NORTH DAKOTA ADVANCE LEGISLATIVE SERVICE > NORTH DAKOTA 63RD LEGISLATIVE ASSEMBLY > CHAPTER 103 > HOUSE BILL 1320

Notice
_____

Added: Text highlighted in green
Deleted: Red text with a strikethrough

Synopsis
_____

AN ACT to amend and reenact section 12.1-17-07 of the North Dakota Century Code, relating to harassment offenses through electronic communications.

Text
_____

BE IT ENACTED BY THE LEGISLATIVE ASSEMBLY OF NORTH DAKOTA:

SECTION 1.

Source: Lexis Advance. Reprinted with permission from Reed Elsevier.

Once you click on this link, all of the session laws for that chapter category will open in a single document. Scroll down to find Chapter 103. Figure 7-4 shows the screen shot for part of the session law for which you have been searching.

From the information at the top of the page in Figure 7-4, you learn (as you previously did using Lexis) that the bill that was passed and resulted in this session law was House Bill 1320. Next, you see the names of the Representatives and Senators who co-sponsored the bill. The very first part of the bill explains exactly what the bill did—in this case, the bill amended and reenacted Section 12.1-17-07 of the North Dakota Century Code.

Finally, although Figure 7-4 shows only a partial excerpt from the bill, you can see some of the particular changes that were made. For example, in Section 1(a), one of the types of communication required to show harassment was changed from "telephone," which is struck through on the bill, to "electronic communication." To compile a complete legislative history of the harassment statute from its original passage in 1973 to the present, you would want to

Figure 7-3. Chapter Category List from 2013 North Dakota Session Laws

Home | Research Center | Session Laws | Chapter Categories

Chapter Categories

The Chapter Categories is the online version of the Session Laws derived from the printed version of the Session Laws.

Every bill is placed within a category that reflects the general subject matter of that bill. Within a category, bills generally are arranged in ascending order by Century Code section number, and the Laws chapter number is assigned. Thus, Session Laws chapter numbers do not have any relationship to date of enactment.

Selecting the appropriate category will lead you to the bills that are compiled under that category for purposes of publication of the Session Laws.

- Appropriations (Chapters 1–62)
- General Provisions (Chapter 63)
- Aeronautics (Chapter 64)
- Agency (No bills)
- Agriculture (Chapters 65–73)
- Alcoholic Beverages (Chapters 74–76)
- Banks and Banking (Chapters 77–88)
- Building and Loan Associations (No bills)
- Carriage (No bills)
- Contracts and Obligations (No bills)
- Corporations (Chapters 89–91)
- Counties (Chapters 92–96)
- Corrections, Parole, and Probation (Chapters 97–101)
- Criminal Code (Chapters 102–114)
- Debtor and Creditor Relationship (Chapter 115)
- Domestic Relations and Persons (Chapters 116–128)
- Education (Chapters 129–145)
- Elementary and Secondary Education (Chapters 146–163)
- Elections (Chapters 164–176)
- Energy (Chapter 177)
- Fires (Chapter 178)
- Foods, Drugs, Oils, and Compounds (Chapters 179–187)
- Game, Fish, Predators, and Boating (Chapters 188–199)
- Governmental Finance (Chapters 200–202)
- Guaranty, Indemnity, and Suretyship (No bills)
- Health and Safety (Chapters 203–219)
- Highways, Bridges, and Ferries (Chapters 220–222)
- Mental and Physical Illness or Disability (Chapters 223–227)

- Insurance (Chapters 228–238)
- Judicial Branch of Government (Chapters 239–245)
- Judicial Procedure, Civil (Chapters 246–247)
- Judicial Procedure, Criminal (Chapter 248)
- Judicial Procedure, Probate (No bills)
- Uniform Probate Code (Chapters 249–251)
- Judicial Proof (No bills)
- Judicial Remedies (Chapters 252–253)
- County Justice Court (No bills)
- Labor and Employment (Chapters 254–255)
- Liens (Chapters 256–259)
- Livestock (Chapter 260–261)
- Military (Chapters 262–276)
- Mining and Gas and Oil Production (Chapters 277–280)
- Motor Vehicles (Chapters 281–311)
- Municipal Government (Chapters 312–317)
- Uniform Commercial Code (No bills)
- Nuisances (No bills)
- Occupations and Professions (Chapters 318–336)
- Offices and Officers (Chapters 337–342)
- Partnerships (Chapter 343)
- Printing Laws (Chapter 344)
- Property (Chapters 345–355)
- Public Buildings (Chapters 356–358)
- Public Utilities (Chapters 359–366)
- Public Welfare (Chapters 367–387)
- Sales and Exchanges (Chapters 388–390)
- Social Security (Chapters 391–394)

- Sports and Amusements (Chapters 395–398)
- State Government (Chapters 399–437)
- State Historical Society and State Parks (Chapter 438)
- Taxation (Chapters 439–475)
- Townships (Chapters 476–477)
- Trusts (No bills)
- Warehousing and Deposits (No bills)
- Waters (Chapters 478–490)
- Weapons (Chapters 491–497)
- Weeds (No bills)
- Weights, Measures, and Grades (No bills)
- Workforce Safety and Insurance (Chapters 498–505)
- Vetoed Measures (Chapters 506–508)
- Measures Approved Over Governor's Veto (No measures)
- Initiated Measures Approved (Chapters 509–510)
- Initiated Measures Disapproved (Chapters 511–513)
- Referred Measures Approved (Chapter 514)
- Referred Measures Disapproved (No measures)
- Constitutional Amendments Approved (Chapters 515–517)
- Constitutional Amendments Disapproved (No amendments)
- Constitutional Amendments Proposed (Chapters 518–522)
- House Concurrent Resolutions (Chapters 523–542)
- House Memorial Resolutions (Chapter 559)
- House Resolutions (No resolutions)
- Senate Concurrent Resolutions (Chapters 543–558)
- Senate Memorial Resolutions (Chapter 560)
- Senate Resolutions (No resolutions)
- Senate Concurrent Memorial Resolutions (No resolutions)

Source: http://www.legis.nd.gov/research-center/session-laws/chapter-categories-18.

look for changes like this that were made in all subsequent amendments to the bill, by looking up each of the session law citations provided in the "History" or "Credits" section of the annotated code.

Once you find the bill number (or numbers) of interest to you, be sure to write it down. The bill number is your access point to many other sources of legislative history.

2. Legislative Assembly Standing Committee Records

Recall that every proposed bill is assigned to a committee for a recommendation before appearing before the full House or Senate. The North Dakota Legislative Branch provides committee records for bills back to 2001 on its website. The information provided in these histories varies by bill, but, in general, you can expect to find the name of the committee that was charged with working on the bill, committee minutes, votes and testimony, and proposed amendments.

To access these materials from the North Dakota Legislative Branch website home page, click on "Research Center" at the bottom of the page. Then, click on "Legislative Bill Histories." From there, select the correct year and chamber. For example, the amendment to the harassment statute in the previous example was passed in 2013 and was numbered HB 1320. Therefore, under the heading

Figure 7-4. Session Law Excerpt on North Dakota Legislative Branch Website

Chapter 103   Criminal Code

CHAPTER 103

HOUSE BILL NO. 1320

(Representatives Kreun, Delmore, Hatlestad, N. Johnson)
(Senators Hogue, Laffen, Sorvaag)

AN ACT to amend and reenact section 12.1-17-07 of the North Dakota Century Code, relating to harassment offenses through electronic communications.

BE IT ENACTED BY THE LEGISLATIVE ASSEMBLY OF NORTH DAKOTA:

SECTION 1. AMENDMENT. Section 12.1-17-07 of the North Dakota Century Code is amended and reenacted as follows:

12.1-17-07. Harassment.

1. A person is guilty of an offense if, with intent to frighten or harass another, the person:

   a. Communicates in writing or by ~~telephone~~electronic communication a threat to inflict injury on any person, to any person's reputation, or to any property;

   b. Makes a telephone call anonymously or in offensively coarse language;

   c. Makes repeated telephone calls or other electronic communication, whether or not a conversation ensues, with no purpose of legitimate communication; or

   d. Communicates a falsehood in writing or by ~~telephone~~electronic communication and causes mental anguish.

2. The offense is a class A misdemeanor if it is under subdivision a of

Source: http://www.legis.nd.gov/assembly/63-2013/session-laws/documents/crmlc.pdf.

for "63rd Assembly— 2013," you would click on "2013 House Bill and Resolution History." All of the bills that were proposed in a given year are listed in chronological order. Simply click on the bill number HB 1320 to access a pdf document containing the bill's history and supplemental documents.

Committee records have also been made available in print since 1959. The name of the print publication is *North Dakota Legislative Assembly House and Senate Standing Committee Minutes.*

3. House and Senate Journals

The daily activities of the House of Representatives and the Senate are recorded in the House and Senate journals. These journals include entries for matters such as the first and second readings of bills, referrals to committees, committee reports and recommendations, and consideration of amendments. Remarks of Representatives and Senators may also be included, but only if requested by the Representative or Senator. Finally, Governor's statements, such as signing statements and veto messages, when available, are also published in the House and Senate journals.

The *Journal of the House* and *Journal of the Senate* have both been published in print since the creation of the state in 1889. An *Index to the Journals of the Senate and House*, organized by bill number, is published each year.

Additionally, the journals are available on the North Dakota Legislative Branch website back to 1997; the combined index is available back to 2001. However, finding these publications is not intuitive; the following example shows how to find references to the 2013 bill mentioned in the previous section, HB 1320. From the Legislative Branch home page, click on the link for "Legislative Assembly," which will take you to a chronological list of legislative sessions; click on the link for "63rd Assembly (2013-2014)." Next, click on the link for "63rd Regular (2013)." Scroll down to find the topic heading "House Journal" and click on the link for the "Combined Journal Index."[9] On the resulting screen, scroll down until you find the correct bill number, HB 1320.[10] (It might be quicker to use your computer's find function.) Because multiple actions are typically taken on a bill, occurring on different days, there are often several listings for each bill. The columns next to the bill number explain the action that was taken and provide the page in the *Journal of the House* or the *Journal of the Senate* where that action was recorded. If the page is from the *Journal of the House*, it is preceded by the letters HJ; if it is from the *Journal of the Senate*, it is preceded by the letters SJ.

Figure 7-5 shows the portion of the journal index where HB 1320 is listed. As you can see from the screen shot, HB 1320 appears in both journals multiple times, with links provided to the pages of the journal in question. However, when you click on the link, you will be brought to the first page in the journal for the date on which the action occurred, which may not be the page on which the action you are looking for is recorded. Simply scroll to the correct page, listed in the index.

---

9. For years prior to 2011, there is no separate link for the Journal Index. Instead, click on "House Journal" or "Senate Journal." The next page will include a dropdown menu from which the index can be chosen.

10. The bills are listed in numerical order, and the House bills are listed before the Senate bills.

Figure 7-5. Excerpt from House Journal Index on the North Dakota Legislative Branch Website

HB 1319	Not concurred	HJ1591
HB 1319	Passed	HJ827 SJ1305 HJ2231
HB 1319	Received from House	SJ648
HB 1319	Reconsidered	HJ2245
HB 1319	Rereferred	HJ505 SJ1057
HB 1319	Returned to House	HJ1424
HB 1320	Amendments adopted	HJ289
HB 1320	Committee report	HJ285 SJ882
HB 1320	Delivered to Governor	HJ1463
HB 1320	Governor signed	HJ1517
HB 1320	Introduced	HJ133 SJ350
HB 1320	Passed	HJ310 SJ894
HB 1320	President signed	SJ964
HB 1320	Received from House	SJ230
HB 1320	Returned to House	HJ1113
HB 1320	Speaker signed	HJ1171
HB 1321	Committee report	HJ315 SJ756

Source: http://www.legis.nd.gov/assembly/63-2013/journals/master-index.html.

According to the index shown in Figure 7-5, committee reports were delivered in both the House and Senate. The index indicates that the committee report delivered in the House appears on HJ285. By clicking on the link for that page number and scrolling until you find page 285, you can find the committee report. Figure 7-6 shows page 285; note that the committee report for HB 1320 is near the bottom.

4. Legislative Management Documents

As noted in Part III.A.1, certain legislative history documents in North Dakota may be produced before a bill is actually introduced. These documents

Figure 7-6. Excerpt from House Journal on the North Dakota Legislative Branch Website

17th DAY   WEDNESDAY, JANUARY 30, 2013   285

on the Sixth order on the calendar.

Page 1, line 9, remove "appointed by the majority leader"

Page 1, line 9, replace the underscored comma with " and"

Page 1, line 9, remove the second "appointed"

Page 1, line 10, remove "by the majority leader"

Page 1, line 10, after "representatives" insert "appointed by the chairman of the legislative management"

Renumber accordingly

REPORT OF STANDING COMMITTEE

HB 1270: Industry, Business and Labor Committee (Rep. Keiser, Chairman) recommends **AMENDMENTS AS FOLLOWS** and when so amended, recommends **DO PASS** (11 YEAS, 3 NAYS, 1 ABSENT AND NOT VOTING). HB 1270 was placed on the Sixth order on the calendar.

Page 1, line 1, remove the second "and"

Page 1, line 2, after "application" insert "; and to declare an emergency"

Page 3, after line 13, insert:

"SECTION 7. EMERGENCY. This Act is declared to be an emergency measure."

Renumber accordingly

REPORT OF STANDING COMMITTEE

HB 1280: Judiciary Committee (Rep. K. Koppelman, Chairman) recommends **AMENDMENTS AS FOLLOWS** and when so amended, recommends **DO PASS** (14 YEAS, 0 NAYS, 0 ABSENT AND NOT VOTING). HB 1280 was placed on the Sixth order on the calendar.

Page 2, line 4, overstrike "a class C felony" and insert immediately thereafter "an offense"

Page 2, line 5, overstrike "to enter, modify,"

Page 2, overstrike lines 6 and 7

Page 2, line 8, overstrike "is the individual or is acting with the authorization or consent of the individual" and insert immediately thereafter "without the authorization or consent of the individual, in order to interfere with or initiate a contract or service for a person other than that individual, to obtain or continue employment, to gain access to personal identifying information of another individual, or to commit an offense in violation of the laws of this state, regardless of whether there is any actual economic loss to the individual. A first offense under this subsection is a class A misdemeanor. A second or subsequent offense under this subsection is a class C felony"

Renumber accordingly

REPORT OF STANDING COMMITTEE

HB 1320: Judiciary Committee (Rep. K. Koppelman, Chairman) recommends **AMENDMENTS AS FOLLOWS** and when so amended, recommends **DO PASS** (12 YEAS, 0 NAYS, 2 ABSENT AND NOT VOTING). HB 1320 was placed on the Sixth order on the calendar.

Page 2, line 4, overstrike "911" and insert immediately thereafter "emergency"

Renumber accordingly

Source: http://www.legis.nd.gov/assembly/63-2013/journals/hr-dailyjnl-17.pdf#pagemode=bookmarks&Page285.

arise from the committee meetings, hearings, and reports conducted by and produced by the Legislative Management.

Legislative Management[11] background memoranda and committee meeting minutes have been published since 1945 in the *North Dakota Legislative Management Background Memorandums and Interim Committee Minutes.* They are also currently available back to 1997 on the North Dakota Legislative Branch website, and older years are expected to be added in the future. From the home page, click on "Legislative Management," and then click the appropriate legislative session. This will take you to a page where minutes and memoranda from various days are collected under separate links. Note that there is not a particularly easy way to figure out which day the proposed bill you are looking for was discussed; rather, you will likely need to click through a few links before you find relevant information.

Legislative Management Final Reports have been published in print as *Report of the North Dakota Legislative Council* since 1971. Earlier reports have been published since 1946 as *Report of the Legislative Research Committee.* Two comprehensive indexes for these publications have been published: *Subject Index to the North Dakota Legislative Council Reports, 1947–1999* and *Subject Index to the North Dakota Legislative Council Reports, 2001–.* Legislative Management Final Reports are also available on the North Dakota Legislative Branch Assembly webpage back to 1997 under the "Legislative Management" link provided on the home page.

IV. Bill Tracking

As noted in Part I, bill tracking is the act of tracking a new proposed bill as it makes its way through the legislative process. This research is often done to keep up with possible or anticipated changes in the law.

The North Dakota Legislative Branch offers a free bill-tracking service. To access this service, you must register and create an ID and password. Once registered, you can search for and add bills to a "tracking list." For each bill, you will be able to see such information as a calendar showing upcoming events, details on committee and conference committee hearings, and bill

---

11. Remember, especially when looking for pre-2009 documents, that the Legislative Management has also been known in the past as the Legislative Council and Legislative Research Committee.

status. The North Dakota Legislative Branch website publishes a comprehensive user manual explaining how to use the system.[12]

---

12. The manual is available at http://www.legis.nd.gov/files/documents/bill-tracking-user-manual.pdf?20150808192415.

Chapter 8

Administrative Law

I. Introduction

Like the federal government, North Dakota has three branches of government: executive, legislative, and judicial. The previous two chapters explained how to research legal authority created by the North Dakota legislative branch, and subsequent chapters will explain how to research legal authority created by the judicial branch. That leaves the legal materials created by the executive branch, which is the topic of this chapter.

The body of law that is made and enforced by the executive branch is referred to as *administrative law*.[1] The executive branch of the state is headed by the Governor, but most administrative law is created and enforced by the wide array of executive agencies[2] that make up the rest of the executive branch. Each agency is charged with governing in a specific subject area. For example, the North Dakota Department of Labor and Human Rights is responsible for implementing and enforcing anti-discrimination laws, and the North Dakota Insurance Department regulates the insurance industry.

Agencies are granted power by the legislature, and the powers they have (sometimes referred to as "quasi" powers) mimic the powers of the other branches of government. For example, quasi-legislative power refers to an agency's ability to make rules that have the force of law, and quasi-executive power refers to an agency's abilities to engage in such matters as investigating rule violations and issuing licenses. Some agencies are also granted quasi-judicial power, which allows them to decide disputes.

---

1. Administrative law may also refer to the body of law addressing the authority and legitimacy of executive-branch lawmaking. This type of administrative law will not be discussed in this book.

2. Note that some administrative agencies are called by other names, such as "departments," "commissions," or "boards."

**Table 8-1. Sample List of Subject Areas Likely to
Require Administrative Law Research**

Banking	Oil and Gas
Business and Commerce	Securities Law
Environmental Law	Tax
Health	Telecommunications
Insurance	Utilities
Labor and Employment	

Administrative law is a vast and important body of law. In fact, for some subject areas that are heavily regulated, such as employment law and environmental law, administrative law comes into play at least as often as statutes and cases. Table 8-1 lists a sampling of subject areas for which researching administrative law is particularly essential.

The forms of administrative law most commonly used by legal researchers are administrative rules and decisions. The next two parts of the chapter are devoted to those materials, and Table 8-2 outlines an effective research process for those materials. Other forms of administrative law that may be of interest to the legal researcher are Attorney General opinions and Governor-created documents, both of which are covered later in this chapter.

Table 8-2. Outline of the Research Process for Administrative Law

1. Identify the administrative agency that controls the subject area and gather background information on the agency.

2. Locate and read rules in the *North Dakota Administrative Code* (N.D.A.C.).

    a. Use the *North Dakota Century Code* (N.D.C.C.) to locate the agency's enabling act or other relevant statutes.

    b. Use secondary sources to identify citations either to the N.D.A.C. or to other primary authority that may lead to N.D.A.C. citations.

    c. Research in the N.D.A.C. itself by browsing the table of contents or performing a keyword search on Lexis or Westlaw.

3. Ensure that rules are current using Shepard's or KeyCite.

4. Check for any proposed rules affecting your subject area.

5. Locate and read agency decisions, if available.

6. Conduct case research to determine if relevant agency decisions have been appealed.

II. Administrative Rules

Administrative rules[3] form the cornerstone of administrative law. Rules are somewhat analogous to statutes in the sense that they lay out rights and responsibilities and have the force of law. However, there are two key differences. First, rules are promulgated (i.e., created) by administrative agencies, which derive their law-making power from the legislature. The legislature delegates this power because certain subjects require more expertise and detail than would be appropriate for statutory law. Thus, rules are typically far more detailed than statutes and may address extremely technical matters.

Second, the rule-making process is very different from the legislative process. While legislatures are elected bodies that derive their law-making power directly from the constitution, administrative agencies are not composed of elected officials and have no such inherent power. Therefore, additional procedures exist to ensure that the rule-making process remains democratic. That process is described in the next section.

A. The Rule-Making Process

The rule-making process for administrative rules in North Dakota is fairly similar to that in the federal government. The process in North Dakota is codified in the Administrative Agencies Practice Act.[4] According to the provisions of that Act, when an agency drafts new rules, those rules must go through a notice and comment process before they become effective. This means that, before a new rule can be adopted, the agency must provide the public with notice of the proposed rule and an opportunity to comment on the rule. In North Dakota, the notice must include such information as an explanation of the proposed rule and its purpose; where the full text of the rule can be viewed; how, when, and where comments can be submitted; the proposed effective date of the rule; and whether the rule is likely to "impact the regulated community in excess of $50,000."[5] Agencies are required to publish an abbreviated notice of the proposed rule in all official county newspapers in the state and to file all materials with the Legislative Council. For substantive rules, a public hearing is also required, followed by at least ten days for additional comments.

The agency is required to consider all written and oral comments received on the proposed rule before promulgating the final rule. Each final rule must

---

3. Rules are also sometimes referred to as *regulations*.
4. N.D.C.C. § 28-32-01 to -52.
5. Office of Attorney General, *Administrative Rules Manual* 5 (2013).

be submitted to the Attorney General for a determination of the rule's legality. Once the rule has been approved by the Attorney General and adopted by the agency, it must be filed, along with the Attorney General's opinion, written comments, and a summary of oral comments, with the Legislative Council so that it can be published in the *North Dakota Administrative Code*. The rules then become effective in accordance with a schedule governed by statute.[6]

B. Researching Rules

1. The *North Dakota Administrative Code*

The official publication for rules is the *North Dakota Administrative Code* (N.D.A.C.). The best way to understand how the N.D.A.C. is organized is to look at how rules are cited. Rules are designated by four numbers separated by hyphens. For example, the citation for the rule addressing applicant eligibility for the Developmental Disabilities Loan Program is N.D. Admin. Code 75-04-03-03 (2015). This citation means that this rule is located at Title 75, Article 4, Chapter 3, Section 3 of the N.D.A.C. Each title corresponds to an agency; for example, Title 75 includes rules promulgated by the Department of Human Services.

Occasionally, you will also come across a rule citation that includes a decimal point. The decimal point may appear in any part of the citation — title, article, chapter, or section number. This simply means that there has been an addition to the code between consecutively numbered areas.

Each rule in the N.D.A.C. is followed by three explanatory notes. These explanatory notes are labeled History, General Authority, and Law Implemented. The History note provides the date the rule was enacted as well as the enactment date of subsequent amendments, if any. The General Authority note provides the citation to the statute or statutes that authorized the agency to promulgate the rule. Finally, the Law Implemented note provides the citation to the statute or statutes that the rule implements. Note that sometimes citations in the General Authority or Law Implemented notes come from federal law or case law. This means that the authority for the agency to promulgate the rule or the law the rule implements is derived from federal law or case law rather than from a state statute.

---

6. *See* N.D.C.C. § 28-32-15(2). The statute specifies specific months for effectiveness, which vary based on the month the rule was filed, but, generally speaking, rules will become effective two to four months after they are filed with the Legislative Council.

Figure 8-1. Regulation in North Dakota Administrative Code

NDAC 75-04-03-03

75-04-03-03. Applicant eligibility.

Application for participation in the developmental disabilities facility loan program will be considered by the department upon a showing that the applicant:

1. Proposes the acquisition, construction, or reconstruction of a facility located in a community identified by the department as a designated area of program development;

2. Is in compliance with the application and submission requirements of the Bank of North Dakota;

3. Is in compliance with the certificate of need requirements of the department of health;

4. Proposes a site approved by local zoning authorities;

5. Proposes a facility for acquisition supported by an appraisal prepared by a certified appraiser;

6. Is a nonprofit entity pursuant to the laws of this state and the United States;

7. Has a governing board whose members live in the geographical area in which the facility or facilities are located;

8. Has a governing board whose members consist of at least one-third consumers or representative of consumers; and

9. Possesses effective control of land, upon which construction is proposed, and buildings to be reconstructed.

History: Effective April 1, 1982; amended effective May 1, 1984.

General Authority: NDCC 6-09.6-02, 50-06-16

Law Implemented: NDCC 6-09.6

Source: Westlaw. Reprinted with permission of Thomson Reuters.

Figure 8-1 shows N.D. Admin. Code 75-04-03-03 (2015), including the explanatory notes.

2. Gathering Background Information

Unless you are familiar with your legal issue or already have a citation to the N.D.A.C., you will likely need to begin your research by gathering background information. The best way to go about gathering background information depends on what you already know.

If you are unsure which agency governs your area, your best bet may be to do a quick Google search. All of North Dakota's agencies have a web presence, and while a Google search may not get you exactly where you need to go on the first try, it will likely help you make an educated guess as to where to look further.

Another option is to browse the Agency Index available on the North Dakota state government website. The Agency Index is an alphabetical index of every agency in North Dakota. The Index itself does not provide information on what each agency covers, but you can often tell by the name of the agency, and each name links directly to that agency's website.

Secondary sources may also help you to figure out which agency governs your issue. Legal encyclopedias like *American Jurisprudence 2d* or *Corpus Juris Secundum* are a good place to start when you need a general overview of your issue. *American Law Reports* annotations and law review articles may also be useful. While you may or may not find citations to specific North Dakota rules, these sources may mention federal administrative agencies or other states' administrative agencies that govern your issue in other jurisdictions. You can then look for a similarly named agency in North Dakota.

Once you have determined which agency governs your particular issue, you should spend some time familiarizing yourself with the work of that agency. This is best done via the agency's website. Although each agency website is different, most provide a wealth of information on the areas of the agency's coverage. Many publish their rules on their websites, and some include other helpful materials such as recent agency decisions, recent orders, and short guides and handbooks that help to explain the work of the agency in layman's terms.

3. Methods of Finding Relevant Citations to the N.D.A.C.

Once you know which agency governs your area of law, there are a variety of methods you might use to locate relevant citations to the N.D.A.C. Note that if you are researching online, going directly to the code is often not the best method. Although the print version of the N.D.A.C. has a general index arranged by topic, that index is not currently available in any of the online services. Additionally, the substance of many rules can be quite intricate and technical so conducting full text searches can be difficult. Therefore, you will likely be more successful if you start with one of the other methods discussed.

The following suggested methods for locating N.D.A.C. citations assume that you have already determined which agency governs your issue. However, if you are still unsure, the following methods will also help you find out that information, though it may take a bit longer than if you gathered that background information in advance.

a. *Starting with the* North Dakota Century Code

The easiest way to find citations to North Dakota rules is to use an annotated version of the *North Dakota Century Code*. As explained in more detail in Chapter 6, the N.D.C.C. is the publication containing North Dakota statutes. Annotated versions are available on both Lexis and Westlaw as well as in print. Annotations provide citations to rules implementing and affected by a given statute.

Although indirect, researching the N.D.C.C. is a good starting point because its index is more comprehensive than that of the N.D.A.C. making it easier to locate relevant statutes that can then lead to relevant rules. Additionally, every agency must be granted the authority for promulgating rules by state statute. This authority is granted in an *enabling act*, which lays out the matters the agency may regulate. If you have a citation to an agency's enabling act, the annotations will lead to citations in the N.D.A.C. that may provide a jumping off point for further research.

Furthermore, Westlaw's version of the N.D.A.C. includes a "Table of Laws Implemented." This table lists citations to rules organized by citations to the state statute or other authority (such as the state constitution or a case) that the rule implements. Once you have a citation to a relevant state statute, therefore, you can use this table to look up citations to rules implementing that statute.

b. *Starting with Secondary Sources*

Because of the dearth of North Dakota-specific secondary sources, it may be difficult to locate citations to the N.D.A.C. in secondary sources. However, they should not be overlooked because they may provide citations to other primary authority that can then lead to citations to the N.D.A.C. For example, you may find a relevant case, and then, when you look up that case, the court may cite a rule or the annotations may refer to a rule. Additionally, researching in secondary sources will help you to understand the subject matter that you are researching and develop more accurate search terms, which you may then use to search directly in the N.D.A.C.

c. *Starting with the N.D.A.C.*

You can research rules directly in the N.D.A.C. itself using a couple of different techniques. First, the table of contents consists of all of the titles in the N.D.A.C., so you can browse this list for the agency that you're looking for, and then browse the articles, chapters, and sections within that title. Each title corresponds to an agency, and title numbers are, for the most part, assigned alphabetically. The N.D.A.C. and its table of contents are available for free on the North Dakota Legislative Branch website.[7] The N.D.A.C. is also available in print and in a CD-ROM version that you can subscribe to through the Secretary of State. Also, don't forget that many state agencies publish their rules directly on their websites, so if you are sure of the agency governing your issue, you may be able to browse relevant provisions of the N.D.A.C. there as well.

Another technique is to use the N.D.A.C. that is available on Lexis and Westlaw. Both services provide both the table of contents and also allow full text searching directly in the code. To access the N.D.A.C. on Lexis, use the browse feature to narrow by "Sources," then "Jurisdiction," then "North Dakota." From here, scroll down to find the N.D.A.C. On Westlaw, first click on "State Materials," then "North Dakota," then scroll down to find the database "North Dakota Regulations."

d. Ensuring that Rules Are Current

After identifying and reading relevant rules, ensure that they are current using either Shepard's on Lexis or KeyCite on Westlaw. Shepard's and KeyCite may also lead you to additional N.D.A.C. citations.

4. Researching Proposed Rules

To research in an area that is heavily regulated, you may also want to track proposed rules. Administrative law changes much more quickly than statutory law does, so it is a good idea to keep abreast of any changes that may be in the works. Proposed rules that have not yet been implemented can be found at the North Dakota Legislative Assembly's website on the "Agency Rules Information" page,[8] organized into a calendar based on meetings and hearings that are scheduled. Westlaw also publishes proposed rules. To access them, go into the N.D.A.C. table of contents, and then click on the link for "North Dakota Proposed And Adopted Regulations" on the right.

Recent rules—those that have been adopted but are not yet effective or that became effective after the last update to the N.D.A.C.—are published in the *Administrative Rules Supplement*, which is available on the North Dakota Legislative Branch's website.[9] These rules can also be found in Westlaw's "North Dakota Proposed and Adopted Regulations" database.

---

7. The web page containing the table of contents is located at http://www.legis.nd.gov/agency-rules/north-dakota-administrative-code.

8. *See* http://www.legis.nd.gov/agency-rules.

9. *See* http://www.legis.nd.gov/agency-rules/administrative-rules-supplement.

III. Administrative Decisions

In addition to having quasi-legislative power, administrative agencies also often have quasi-judicial power; that is, they have the power to decide disputes involving the enforcement of their rules. A dispute may arise after an agency decision, such as the denial of an application for a license, or it may result from a citizen filing a complaint with the agency against another person or business. Unless the dispute is resolved in an informal manner, such as through negotiation or mediation, a hearing will then be held. The hearing will be presided over either by an agency hearing officer or an Administrative Law Judge (ALJ). The hearing officer or ALJ will hear evidence, and then make findings of facts and issue a decision.

Agency decisions are appealable to state district courts. Therefore, if you find an agency decision of interest, you should always research other case law, using the techniques described in Chapter 11, to see if it has been appealed. Note that, although agency decisions usually have little if any precedential value, courts will sometimes grant them some deference, depending on the agency in question.

North Dakota state administrative decisions are extraordinarily difficult to locate. While some states have a systematic manner for publishing some or all of their state's administrative decisions, in North Dakota, there is no central publication for such decisions, and very few are available on Lexis or Westlaw.[10] Your best bet is to check with the website of the agency in question to see if it publishes recent decisions online. Be aware that, in most instances, you will be unable to perform general research in agency decisions. Nonetheless, if you know that a particular decision has been issued, you may be able to request a copy of it through the specific agency.

IV. Researching North Dakota Attorney General Opinions

The North Dakota Attorney General acts as chief legal counsel in the state, providing legal representation and advising the state on legal matters. Among other duties, the Attorney General issues written opinions in response to legal

---

10. Both Lexis and Westlaw currently have databases containing decisions of the North Dakota Public Service Commission (called the "North Dakota Public Utilities Commission" on Lexis Advance). Additionally, Lexis has a database containing securities-related decisions in a database called "N.D. Office of Commerce of Securities."

questions posed by public officials, administrative agencies, and state and local officials. Attorney General opinions have the force of law until and unless they are overruled by the legislature or a court. They are not binding on the courts, but they are typically accorded significant consideration. By law, the North Dakota Attorney General may issue opinions only to certain state and city officials (including state agencies and the legislature) as well as a few other designated state boards and organizations.[11] If a state official acts on information provided in an Attorney General opinion, that official is protected from liability.

Prior to 2002, the Attorney General also issued "advisory letters." Advisory letters held the same legal weight as opinions but were issued for matters that had a regional or otherwise limited impact rather than a statewide impact. In 2002, the Attorney General discontinued issuing advisory letters, and now such matters are also addressed in opinions.

North Dakota Attorney General opinions dating back to 1942 and advisory letters dating back to 1951 are available for free on the North Dakota Attorney General's web page by clicking on the link for "Legal Opinions."[12] The opinions and letters can be browsed by year or searched by keyword. The site also has a "Cumulative Index of Opinions," organized by subjected.

Opinions dating back to 1969 are available on Lexis in the "N.D. Attorney General Opinions" database. Opinions dating back to 1977 are available on Westlaw, though finding them is not entirely intuitive. You must first click on "State Materials," then "North Dakota," then "North Dakota Administrative Opinions and Orders." Within this last link is another link for "Attorney General Opinions." Opinions are also available in print; coverage depends on the library in question.

Older opinions are a bit more difficult to find. Those back to 1924 are available on microfiche, though, again, coverage varies by library. Additionally, you may request an older opinion by contacting the North Dakota Attorney General's Office directly.

---

11. Attorneys General may issue opinions to the following categories of individuals/organizations: "state officers, state agencies, the state legislature, county state's attorneys, city attorneys, city governing bodies, water resource boards, soil conservation districts, health district boards, the Judicial Conduct Commission, and the Garrison Diversion Conservancy District." *See* Office of Attorney General, *A Guide to Attorney General Opinions* (2012), available at http://www.ag.nd.gov/Brochures/Fact-Sheet/AGOpinions.pdf.
12. *See* http://www.ag.nd.gov/index.shtml.

V. Researching North Dakota Governor Documents

The Governor is the chief executive officer in the state. In this capacity, the Governor is empowered by the state Constitution and statutes to implement executive authority via a variety of documents. The most important of these documents in researching administrative law are executive orders and proclamations.

Executive orders are documents issued by the Governor that have the force of law. Executive orders may be issued on a variety of matters, such as implementing emergency powers, creating committees or commissions, or addressing certain administrative issues. For example, on April 1, 2015, the North Dakota Governor issued an executive order declaring a fire emergency in the state and instituting a statewide burn ban in certain designated areas.

Governor proclamations are more ceremonial in nature. For example, on June 7, 2015, the North Dakota Governor issued a proclamation declaring that day "Cancer Survivors Day."

North Dakota executive orders are available for free back to 1963 on the North Dakota Governor's web page under the "Media Center" link.[13] Recent executive orders appear directly on the web page under that link while older ones may be accessed via a second link called "Executive Orders Archive." Proclamations are available in the same place back to December of 2010. Executive orders and proclamations are organized on the website by year. There is a search box as well, but note that it searches the entire site rather than exclusively searching the executive orders and proclamations.

Executive orders and proclamations are also available in print, but publication is irregular and coverage depends on the library in question. Use your library's catalog to search for "North Dakota Executive Orders" or "North Dakota Governor Proclamations." There is no easy way to locate older executive orders or proclamations. The best method is to contact the State Historical Society,[14] which archives many of these documents and provides reference services, including the ability to email an archivist for help if you are unable to conduct in-person research in Bismarck.

---

13. *See* http://governor.nd.gov/media-center.
14. *See* http://history.nd.gov/archives/stateagencies/governor.html.

Chapter 9

Court Rules and Rules of Professional Conduct

I. Introduction

The prior chapters discussed a large portion of the major primary law in North Dakota. Subsequent chapters of the book delve into another hugely important area of research — case law research.

However, when practicing law, it is not enough to simply understand the substantive law; lawyers must also understand the rules of the court in which they practice. These include rules governing both procedure and evidence, and failing to follow these rules can be damaging, even fatal, to a case.

Additionally, because of the important and sensitive nature of the profession, lawyers are held to a high standard of ethics, laid down in rules of professional conduct (also sometimes referred to as rules of professional responsibility). A lawyer who fails to abide by the rules of professional conduct may face discipline and could even lose the privilege to practice law.

This chapter will assist you in locating and interpreting both court rules and the rules governing professional conduct in North Dakota.

II. Types of Rules

A. Court Rules

Court rules are promulgated by courts to govern appropriate practice and procedure by attorneys appearing in those courts. Most courts have multiple layers of rules, and lawyers must understand them all. Some rules apply to all courts in the state, others to specific levels of courts, and still others only to a particular court or courts in a given jurisdiction.

Court rules have the force of law. Therefore, understanding and following the rules of your court is as essential to a positive outcome in your client's case as having the substantive law on your side.

1. Rules of Procedure

Among the most familiar court rules are the Federal Rules of Civil Procedure. However, the Federal Rules of Civil Procedure are only one of a myriad set of rules that you might come across in practice and are only applicable to certain federal courts. States also have their own rules of procedure. These rules often mirror the federal rules, but they are not identical; therefore, you must know the rules of procedure applicable to your particular jurisdiction and court.

When you are practicing in North Dakota state courts, multiple sets of procedural rules may apply, depending on the court in which you are practicing. The most generally applicable are the North Dakota Rules of Court; these are applicable to all courts in the state, except where a separate appellate or Supreme Court rule or order applies. The North Dakota Rules of Court cover such areas as pleadings and motions, the conduct of trials, and the preparation of judgments, orders, and decrees. Some of the rules are quite specific. For example, Rule 10.1(b)(1) provides, "Anyone entering the courtroom while court is in session must immediately be seated. Everyone must behave in a quiet and orderly manner. No person may enter or leave the courtroom while the court is charging the jury, except in an emergency."

In addition to these rules of general applicability, there are special sets of rules governing the practice and procedure in specific types of courts or cases. The North Dakota Rules of Appellate Procedure apply to all cases in the North Dakota Supreme Court. At the trial court level, the North Dakota Rules of Civil Procedure and the North Dakota Rules of Criminal Procedure apply to civil cases and criminal cases respectively. The North Dakota Rules of Juvenile Procedure apply to cases conducted under the Uniform Juvenile Court Act.[1] If you are unsure which set of rules applies to your court, check the "scope" section provided at the beginning of each set of rules.

2. Rules of Evidence

The Federal Rules of Evidence apply to federal trials, but there are also state rules of evidence that mirror, but are not necessarily identical to, the federal rules. In North Dakota, these are called the North Dakota Rules of Evidence.

---

1. *See* N.D. Cent. Code § 27-20-01, *et seq.*

The North Dakota Rules of Evidence apply to all courts in the state and cover such areas as the types of evidence that may be admitted and excluded, how such evidence is admitted and authenticated, and what kind of information is considered privileged and therefore confidential. For example, Rule 504, dealing with the spousal privilege, provides that "[a] communication is confidential if it is made privately by an individual to the individual's spouse and is not intended for disclosure to any other person."

3. Local Rules

Local rules are additional rules handed down by a particular court or a set of courts within a given judicial district. Local rules may cover a variety of matters such as court fees and hours. In addition to the general rules discussed in the previous section, you must know any additional rules laid down by the given court in which you are practicing. In North Dakota, there are eight judicial districts, and each district has a small number of local rules that apply in addition to the rules of general applicability discussed above in Part II.A.1. Most of the local rules in North Dakota concern how cases are assigned to judges.

B. Rules of Professional Conduct

Lawyers are held to a high standard of professional behavior, and every state has its own rules of professional conduct that lawyers must follow. These rules govern the ethical conduct of the practice of law and are essential in maintaining the integrity of the profession and its practitioners. Violating the rules of professional conduct can result in disciplinary action, may open you up to malpractice lawsuits, and can even result in losing your law license.

In North Dakota, these rules are called the North Dakota Rules of Professional Conduct. The rules are often broad and govern a wide array of conduct. For example, Rule 1.1 states, "A lawyer shall provide competent representation to a client. Competent representation requires the legal knowledge, skill, thoroughness and preparation reasonably necessary for the representation." Similarly, Rule 1.3 states, "A lawyer shall act with reasonable diligence and promptness in representing a client."

III. Locating Rules

All of the North Dakota court rules as well as the North Dakota Rules of Professional Conduct are published and freely available on the "Rules" page of the North Dakota Supreme Court website.[2] Figure 9-1 shows a screen shot of the North Dakota Supreme Court's "Rules" page.

Each set of rules begins with a section describing the scope of the rules—the courts in which the given set of rules applies. The content of a given set of rules is generally self-explanatory by its title. The only court rules that will require a small amount of digging are local rules. These rules are located under the heading, "Local Court Procedural and Administrative Rules." Within that heading, local rules are organized by judicial district.

The versions of the rules published for free on the North Dakota Supreme Court website contain some helpful information in addition to the text of the rules. The various types of court rules, including the rules of evidence, contain historical notes on when each rule was passed; references to committee minutes for meetings during which the rule was discussed; explanatory notes, if any; and references to other rules and statutes affected by the rule. Links to documents are provided where the documents are available for free online.

Even more helpful, the Rules of Professional Conduct contain not just the text of the rules, but also the comments of the committees that created the rules. These comments provide further explanation as to what the rule means. For example, recall that Rule 1.3, mentioned earlier in Part II.B, states, "A lawyer shall act with reasonable diligence and promptness in representing a client." This rule is followed by several comments. Comment 2 clarifies, "A lawyer's workload must be controlled so that each matter can be handled competently."

Beyond the North Dakota Supreme Court website, annotated versions of all North Dakota rules are also available on Lexis and Westlaw. Annotated versions contain not just the text and explanatory information discussed in the previous two paragraphs, but also references to other materials such as cases and secondary sources that interpret, discuss, or analyze the rules.

On Lexis, use the browse feature and click on "Sources," then "Jurisdiction," then "North Dakota." From there, scroll down to the "North Dakota Local, State, and Federal Court Rules" database. Links for the individual categories of rules can be found under the table of contents for this database.

On Westlaw, click on "State Materials," then select "North Dakota." Under the heading for "North Dakota Statutes and Rules," there is a link called "North

---

2. The address is http://www.ndcourts.gov/Rules/. Note that there are also rules on this website governing such areas as judicial conduct, continuing legal education, and limited practice of law by law students. This chapter discusses only court rules governing procedure and evidence as well as rules of professional conduct.

Figure 9-1. North Dakota Supreme Court's "Rules" Page

North Dakota Supreme Court Rules ◄▲ ✐?

North Dakota Rules

HOME
OPINIONS
SEARCH
INDEX
GUIDES
LAWYERS
RULES
RESEARCH
COURTS
CALENDAR
NOTICES
NEWS
SELF HELP
SUBSCRIBE
CUSTOMIZE
COMMENTS

Search all Rules:

[   ]

[Execute]   ☐ Use Free-Text Query.
                              Tips for searching

Use Contents to select a Set of Rules to be viewed. All North Dakota Court Rules are available.
The panel to the right can be used to select a particular rule, as can "links" in this frame. Rules "Reserved for future use" are omitted from the panel to the right.
You can begin by selecting a set of rules either below or to the right, or by Searching. All rules can be Searched from this form, or individual Sets of Rules may be Searched by first selecting the Set.

Contents

- Appellate Procedure, North Dakota Rules of
- Civil Procedure, North Dakota Rules of
- Criminal Procedure, North Dakota Rules of
- Juvenile Procedure, North Dakota Rules of
- Evidence, North Dakota Rules of
- Rules of Court, North Dakota
- Local Court Procedural and Administrative Rules
- Administrative Rules and Orders, North Dakota
- Admission to Practice Rules, North Dakota
- Limited Practice of Law by Law Students
- Continuing Legal Education, North Dakota Rules for
- Professional Conduct, North Dakota Rules of
- Lawyer Discipline, North Dakota Rules for
- Standards for Imposing Lawyer Sanctions, North Dakota
- Code of Judicial Conduct, North Dakota
- Judicial Conduct Commission, Rules of the
- Rule on Procedural Rules, Administrative Rules and Administrative Orders of the North Dakota Supreme Court
- Rule on Local Court Procedural Rules and Administrative Rules, North Dakota

Top Home Opinions Search Index Lawyers Rules Research Courts Calendar Comments

Source: https://www.ndcourts.gov/rules/.

Table 9-1. Researching and Analyzing Court Rules and Rules of Professional Conduct: Suggested Steps

1. Locate the rule on the North Dakota Supreme Court website.
2. Read the rule and any explanatory notes.
3. Find the rule in an annotated source.
4. Update the rule.

Dakota State Court Rules." Clicking on this link will take you to hyperlinked tables of contents for all of the various types of rules in the state.

Finally, North Dakota court rules and the Rules for Professional Conduct are available in print in the *North Dakota Century Code* (N.D.C.C.). If you are unsure of whether a given rule exists for a topic, browsing the table of contents for the rules, either in the N.D.C.C. or in one of the online sources above, is usually the easiest method. However, since the rules are published with the N.D.C.C., you can also use the index for that publication to search for rules by topic. In addition to being available in print, that index is available on Westlaw.

IV. Interpreting Rules

Court rules and rules of professional conduct can often appear deceptively simple to understand, unlike many statutes, cases, and administrative regulations. Court rules and rules of professional conduct are often written in concise, straightforward language, many times with concrete, seemingly black and white details. These rules are not always as simple as they appear. Thus, when working with court rules and rules of professional conduct, keep in mind that, just as with other types of law, you may need to analyze and interpret what you find.

Table 9-1 provides a list of suggested steps for researching and analyzing court rules and rules of professional conduct.

First, locate the rule. You may want to start with the North Dakota Supreme Court website because that source is free. If you are unsure of whether a rule exists for your topic, browse the tables of contents. For court rules, be sure to read the "scope" section at the beginning of the rules to ensure that the rules you are looking at apply to your given court.

Next, read the rule carefully, remembering that the text may appear deceptively simple. Also look carefully at any accompanying explanatory notes or comments.

Third, locate the rule in an annotated source. The North Dakota Supreme Court's website does not contain the annotations that are so helpful in understanding, interpreting, or analyzing rules. The rules are annotated in the print version of the *North Dakota Century Code* as well as on Lexis and Westlaw.

If a rule is relatively new to you or is particularly vague or complex, look for annotations providing citations to secondary sources, which may provide background and explain the rule in more detail. Note that, although few North Dakota-specific secondary sources exist, general secondary sources are particularly helpful with court rules and rules of professional conduct since many of the state rules are modeled after federal rules.

Once you feel more comfortable with the rule, look for annotations providing citations to relevant statutes and to any cases that have interpreted the rule. Follow up by reading those sources.

Finally, ensure your rule is up-to-date using Shepard's or KeyCite. These tools are explained in Chapter 12, Updating.

Chapter 10

Judicial Systems and Judicial Opinions

I. Introduction

Chapters 5 through 9 covered how to research enacted law. The other major body of primary legal authority is case law. This chapter addresses the North Dakota judicial system and explains how to read a case effectively. Chapter 11 explains how to research cases.

II. The North Dakota Judicial System

North Dakota's judicial system consists primarily of the North Dakota Supreme Court and the district courts. All judges are selected through non-partisan elections.

A. The North Dakota Supreme Court

There are five justices on the North Dakota Supreme Court, who serve ten-year terms. Their compensation cannot be reduced during their tenure, a check on the pressure the legislature might apply by reducing salaries following politically charged decisions. One of the justices serves as chief justice. The chief justice is the administrative head of the state judicial system.

A unique feature of North Dakota's judicial system is that the Supreme Court typically functions as the sole appellate body. North Dakota does not have a regular intermediate court of appeals. Instead, the Supreme Court can appoint active or retired Supreme Court justices, active or retired district court judges, or lawyers in the state to temporary one-year appointments to the Court of Appeals. The Court of Appeals then hears cases referred to it by the Supreme Court. Some years, the Supreme Court refers no cases to the Court of Appeals.

Another interesting feature of North Dakota's judicial system is that the constitution limits when the Supreme Court can declare a law unconstitutional.

Specifically, the Supreme Court can rule a legislative enactment unconstitutional only if at least four of the five justices agree.[1] In other decisions, a simple majority is sufficient.

B. The District Courts

The district courts are where litigation begins in North Dakota: They have original and general jurisdiction in all cases involving state law. North Dakota is divided into eight judicial districts, and there is a district court in each of North Dakota's fifty-three counties.[2] District judges serve for six-year terms. As with the Supreme Court justices, the compensation of the district judges cannot be reduced during their tenure.

C. Municipal Courts

Finally, the municipal courts hear violations of municipal ordinances. Municipal ordinances cover things like conduct on streets and sidewalks, parking, the maintenance of animals within city limits, land development, etc. For example, Grand Forks Municipal Code § 8-401 prohibits jaywalking, providing that "[b]etween adjacent intersections at which traffic-control signals are in operation, pedestrians shall not cross at any place except in a marked crosswalk." Grand Forks Municipal Code § 11-0102 provides for the licensing of dogs and cats. It provides that "[n]o person, firm, association or corporation shall own, keep, or harbor a dog or cat which is over six (6) months of age without first having obtained a license therefor." Defendants can appeal judgments of conviction in municipal court to the district court. Municipal judges serve four-year terms.

III. North Dakota Reporters

When judicial opinions are published, they are collected and put into a *reporter*, a volume of published cases. This is why published cases are called *reported* cases. West publishes state court decisions in regional reporters, which are groupings of states by region. North Dakota Supreme Court cases are pub-

---

1. N.D. Const. Art. VI, § 4.
2. For a color map of North Dakota's judicial districts, visit www.ndcourts.gov/court/Districts/Districts.htm.

Table 10-1. Regional Reporters and States Included

Atlantic Reporter A., A.2d	Connecticut, Delaware, District of Columbia, Maine, Maryland, New Hampshire, New Jersey, Pennsylvania, Rhode Island, Vermont
North Eastern Reporter N.E., N.E.2d	Illinois, Indiana, Massachusetts, New York, Ohio
North Western Reporter N.W., N.W.2d	Iowa, Michigan, Minnesota, Nebraska, North Dakota, South Dakota, Wisconsin
Pacific Reporter P., P.2d, P.3d	Alaska, Arizona, California, Colorado, Hawaii, Idaho, Kansas, Montana, Nevada, New Mexico, Oklahoma, Oregon, Utah, Washington, Wyoming
South Eastern Reporter S.E., S.E.2d	Georgia, North Carolina, South Carolina, Virginia, West Virginia
South Western Reporter S.W., S.W.2d, S.W.3d	Arkansas, Kentucky, Missouri, Tennessee, Texas
Southern Reporter So., So. 2d, So. 3d	Alabama, Florida, Louisiana, Mississippi

lished in the *North Western Reporter*, the official reporter for North Dakota.[3] For example, the case *Johnson v. State*, 858 N.W.2d 632 (N.D. 2015) can be found in volume 858 of the second series of the *North Western Reporter*, beginning on page 632. The case was decided in 2015.

Also included in the *North Western Reporter* are cases from Iowa, Michigan, Minnesota, Nebraska, South Dakota, and Wisconsin. Notably, volumes of the *North Western Reporter* with only the North Dakota cases included are available in some North Dakota libraries. The other regional reporters published by West, and the states included, are listed in Table 10-1.

Every region has at least two, and some have three, *series* of reporters. When a series reaches a certain number of volumes, West will begin a new series. Therefore, when the *North Western Reporter* reached volume 300, West began the *North Western Reporter, Second Series* (N.W.2d).

West determines which states to include in which reporters. Some of the groupings may initially appear bizarre, such as placing Kentucky in the *South*

---

3. Many states publish their own cases in a state-specific reporter. That reporter is frequently the official reporter for that state.

Western Reporter. West, however, made some of these groupings in the 1800s, before the country was completely settled.

The regional reporter groupings have no legal impact. Additionally, they are not the same as the groupings of states into the federal circuits—groupings that do have legal impact. The Eighth Circuit includes North Dakota, South Dakota, Minnesota, Arkansas, Iowa, Missouri, and Nebraska, but the state court decisions of those states appear in two different regional reporters.

Like most other states, North Dakota does not publish district court decisions. You can obtain district court decisions from the court itself. Alternatively, Westlaw provides selected district court decisions beginning in 2001. Municipal court decisions are not available online.

IV. Reading Cases Effectively

A. The Anatomy of a Reported Case

A case published in print or online through a service like Lexis or Westlaw will have exactly the same language as the decision written by the court.[4] It will also have some enhancements added by the publisher. Either the publisher draws these enhancements from the court record of the case or they are written by the publisher's editorial staff.

In order to best follow the discussion of the anatomy of a case, refer to Figure 10-1 and Appendix 10-1 at the end of the chapter. The figure and appendix show the same case, *Johnson v. State*, but Figure 10-1 illustrates the first screen on Westlaw, while Appendix 10-1 shows the first two pages of the case as it appears in the *North Western Reporter*.

Citation. Both excerpts show the case's citation at the top. Significantly, the citation is different on each. On the Westlaw excerpt in Figure 10-1, you see the citation to the *North Western Reporter* in the national format; on the *North Western Reporter* excerpt, you see the citation in the format preferred by North

---

4. A quick note for law students: The cases you will find through your legal research in law school and in practice will likely look very different from the cases that you will read in your law school casebooks. The cases in your law school casebooks have been heavily edited to focus you on the specific material that teaches the concept that the book is covering. Therefore, a case that actually addresses several issues may be edited down to just one in your casebook. In addition to editing out irrelevant issues and discussion, your casebook editors do not include the publisher's enhancements.

Figure 10-1. Case Excerpt from Westlaw

858 N.W.2d 632
Supreme Court of North Dakota.

Robert L. JOHNSON, Petitioner and Appellant

v.

STATE of North Dakota, Respondent and Appellee.

No. 20140191.   Jan. 15, 2015.   Rehearing Denied Feb. 12, 2015.

Synopsis

Background: Defendant was convicted of simple assault and two counts of contact by bodily fluid or excrement. The Supreme Court reversed and remanded due to instructional error, 2001 ND 184, 636 N.W.2d 391. On remand, defendant was again convicted on the three charges. Defendant applied for postconviction relief, alleging ineffective assistance of counsel. The District Court, Stutsman County, Southeast Judicial District, John T. Paulson, J., dismissed application as untimely. Defendant appealed.

Holdings: The Supreme Court, McEvers, J., held that:

1 trial counsel's letter acknowledging mistakes in moving for a new trial did not constitute newly-discovered evidence that would qualify defendant for an exception to the two-year deadline for filing application for postconviction relief, and

2 defendant waived for appellate review the issue of whether he suffered from a physical disability or mental disease that would qualify him for an exception to the two-year limitations period.

Affirmed.

West Headnotes (6)

⊟

⊞ Change View

1 **Criminal Law** ⊶ Civil or criminal nature
   Criminal Law ⊶ Proceedings
   Postconviction relief proceedings are civil in nature and governed by the Rules of Civil Procedure.

2 **Criminal Law** ⊶ Interlocutory, Collateral, and Supplementary Proceedings and Questions
   Supreme Court reviews an appeal from a summary denial of postconviction relief as it reviews an appeal from a summary judgment.

3 **Criminal Law** ⊶ Necessity for Hearing
   The party opposing the motion for summary disposition is entitled to all reasonable inferences at the preliminary stages of a postconviction proceeding and is entitled to an evidentiary hearing if a reasonable inference raises a genuine issue of material fact.

Source: Westlaw. Reprinted with permission of Thomson Reuters.

Dakota courts, 2015 ND 7, which is called *medium-neutral* citation. 2015 is for the year the case was decided, ND is for the North Dakota Supreme Court, and 7 means that it was the seventh case decided in 2015. When practicing in North Dakota, you must use medium-neutral citation for all cases after January 1, 1997, along with the *North Western Reporter* citation. For cases before January 1, 1997, you will use the *North Western Reporter* citation.[5]

Court. Listed at the top of the Westlaw screen (and just under the caption in the reporter) is the court that decided the case.

5. For more information, see North Dakota Rules of Court 11.6.

Parties and procedural designations. The names of all of the parties appear with their procedural designations (e.g., Appellant). If the party who lost at the trial level has a right to appeal, she will be called the appellant or the petitioner; the party who won at the trial level will be called the appellee or respondent.

Docket number. This is the number assigned to the case by the court. For the *Johnson* case, the docket number is No. 20140191. The docket number is a unique identifier. The majority of documents filed in a case will not be published; having the docket number will allow you to obtain from the court any documents associated with a particular case.

Date. Each case will show the date of decision. Other dates may be shown (e.g., in *Johnson*, a rehearing date is shown), but for citation purposes, only the date of decision is important.

Synopsis. One of the most helpful of the publisher's enhancements, the synopsis gives a short background of the case, including the key facts, procedural posture, points of law, and disposition. The synopsis is helpful to skim to determine whether a case could be relevant to your research. While it is a helpful aid, you cannot cite to it because it is not part of the court's decision.

Headnotes. A headnote is a short numbered statement of a single point of law. Some headnotes are only a sentence; others are a brief paragraph. Many times the text of the headnote comes directly from the opinion; other times, it is summarized by legal editors. The headnotes lay out the points of law from the opinion in order; therefore, they read like an outline of the points of law from the opinion. The text of the opinion is numbered to correspond to the headnotes. As a result, if headnote 3 looks particularly relevant to your search, you can quickly skim the opinion to find headnote 3. If you're online, click the [3] in the headnote, which will then take you directly to that part of the opinion.

Headnotes are key to researching cases. At the very beginning of the headnote, before the summary of the point of law, you'll see a list of key words in an outline-style format. These are part of the publisher's subject indexes, as explained in Chapter 11, Researching Case Law.

Because headnotes are products of legal publishers, their number and content will not be the same from publisher to publisher. So, for example, the headnotes on Lexis will be different from the headnotes on Westlaw. As with the synopsis, you cannot cite to the headnotes because they are not part of the actual opinion.

Procedural information. The name of the judge or justice who wrote the opinion for the court will appear. Following the judge's name will be "J." for judge or justice, or "C.J." for chief judge or chief justice. The procedural information will include whether there are concurring or dissenting opinions. It will also include the attorneys who argued the appeal.

Disposition. The decision of the court to affirm, reverse, remand, or vacate the decision below will be listed. If the appellate court agrees with only part of the lower court's decision, it may affirm in part and reverse in part.

Opinion. Finally, the text of the opinion appears. The name of the judge or justice who wrote the opinion will precede the opinion, and the name will be in all capital letters. If all of the judges do not agree with the opinion, there will be multiple opinions. A judge writes a *concurring opinion* when she agrees with the outcome of the majority opinion, but not necessarily how the majority reached its conclusion. A judge writes a *dissenting opinion* when she disagrees with the majority's reasoning and result. If no opinion garners a majority, then the case is decided by a *plurality decision*, which is the decision that garners the most support. The parts of the opinion itself are discussed in further detail below.

Pagination. When you use the *North West Reporter*, as shown in Appendix 10-1, the pagination is clear. Online providers, like Lexis and Westlaw, transfer opinions from the printed reporter online. While online content does not have page numbers like books do, you still need to be able to identify the different pages of the opinion, even when you're working online. Lexis and Westlaw indicate the page of the opinion by using *star paging*. When a new page in the print reporter begins, Lexis and Westlaw insert an asterisk and the page number, like *634. Note that Lexis and Westlaw frequently give star pagination for multiple reporters. On Lexis, you can select which reporter's pages you want to see at the beginning of the case. When you do, those are the only star pages you will see. Westlaw, on the other hand, differentiates between different reporters by using a different number of asterisks (stars) before the page number. Figure 10-2 shows an example of a case from Westlaw with star paging.

B. Reading Cases

Reading cases the same way you read magazines or novels or even undergraduate textbooks will not serve you well. Instead, reading cases is a learned skill. As with any new skill, it takes guidance, practice, and patience. This section explains the process of reading a case and describes techniques for taking effective notes on what you read. Ultimately, you will be surprised at how intensive the process is. With experience, it will become easier and easier, until it is second nature. But, as seasoned lawyers will attest, even when you have mastered the art of reading and taking notes on a case, it remains the most intensive and time-consuming reading experience you're likely to have.

Figure 10-2. Star Paging

Opinion

McEVERS, Justice.

[¶ 1] Robert L. Johnson appeals from a district court judgment summarily dismissing his application for post-conviction relief. We affirm the district court's summary dismissal of Johnson's post-conviction relief application as untimely.

I

[¶ 2] In 1999, Robert L. Johnson was charged with one count of simple assault and two counts of contact by bodily fluid or excrement. Johnson was tried and convicted of all three counts. Because of improper jury instructions, Johnson's convictions were reversed and remanded in *State v. Johnson*, 2001 ND 184, 636 N.W.2d 391. On August 16, 2002, Johnson was again convicted of all three counts. On December 11, 2002, a judgment of conviction was entered. Johnson appealed to this Court but later withdrew his appeal after accepting a plea bargain agreement pertaining to the disposition of the appealed charges. The court dismissed Johnson's appeal on August 13, 2003. On March 21, 2014, Johnson applied for post-conviction relief alleging ineffective assistance of counsel. In support of his application, Johnson submitted a letter dated July 17, 2013, from Johnson's 2002 trial *634 attorney acknowledging he made some mistakes regarding his representation of Johnson. The State moved to dismiss on the grounds that the time for filing a post-conviction relief application had expired. The district court dismissed Johnson's application as barred by the two-year statute of limitations for post-conviction relief applications. Johnson appealed.

Source: Westlaw. Reprinted with permission of Thomson Reuters.

1. Understanding Unfamiliar Terms and Procedure

When you read cases and encounter unfamiliar terms, *look them up*! In other contexts, you can frequently gloss over unfamiliar words and get the gist of the passage from the surrounding text—and that is good enough. It's not good enough in legal reading, which must be very precise. You must read and understand every word in a passage. So, when you encounter unfamiliar words, pause and look them up in a legal dictionary like *Black's Law Dictionary*. Write the definition in the margin of the case if you have printed it, or annotate it if working online. Writing down the definition will help you remember the meaning of the word, and it will save you time when you re-read the case.

In addition to understanding unfamiliar terms, you have to understand the *procedural posture* of the case you are reading. The procedural posture is the path that the case took to get where it is. The majority of the cases you will encounter in your research are appellate cases. The opinion will tell you how the case ended up on appeal. Four of the more common paths are (1) motion to dismiss; (2) motion for summary judgment; (3) judgment as a matter of law; and (4) trial.

Motion to dismiss. A motion to dismiss resolves the case before it ever goes to trial. A defendant can move to dismiss when it believes that the plaintiff has not stated a valid legal claim in the complaint. In other words, even if all of the facts alleged in the complaint are true, the law doesn't permit a suit based on those facts. In some jurisdictions, this is called a *demurrer*. Parties usually move to dismiss at the very beginning of litigation.

Motion for summary judgment. Summary judgment also resolves the case without a trial. A party can move for summary judgment when it believes that there is no real dispute about the facts of the case, and given those facts, that party is entitled to judgment as a matter of law. Parties usually move for summary judgment towards the end of litigation, after some facts have been determined through depositions, affidavits, and interrogatories, but before trial.

Judgment as a matter of law. When one party has submitted all of its evidence at trial, and the court determines that there is no way that a jury could find for that party, the court can enter judgment as a matter of law. This happens at the close of one side's case in a trial.

Trial. The most obvious path to appeal is after a trial. Sometimes cases are tried by jury; other times they are tried by the judge in a *bench trial*. In a bench trial, the judge both finds the facts and determines the law to reach a final decision.

2. The Parts of a Judicial Opinion

Judges tend to follow the same general format in writing their opinions:

Introductory paragraph. In the first paragraph, the court summarizes the main dispute, identifies the parties, and summarizes the court's holding.

Background. The court will then provide the facts of the case. Sometimes, this section is called "Background" or "Facts." The court usually includes only the key facts and the contextual facts. The key facts are the facts that triggered the court's holding.[6] The contextual facts are necessary for the reader to understand the underlying dispute.

Analysis. The court's analysis is the heart of the opinion. The analysis will frequently follow the IREAC format (Issue, Rule/Explanation, Application, Conclusion).[7] The court will first identify the issue it is resolving. It will then provide the governing law, and it will explain that law. After that, the court will apply the law to the issue before it and reach a conclusion

There are two important products of the court's analysis, and knowing the difference between them is crucial. The first is the *holding*. A holding is the court's answer to the specific issue presented by the parties. The holding will always be articulated using the facts of the case before the court. The second is the *legal principle of the case* or the *rule of the case*. This is the general legal rule that a reader can extract from the court's analysis in this particular case.

---

6. The term "trigger facts" is from Coughlin et al., *A Lawyer Writes* (2d ed. 2013).

7. Other variations of this format include CREAC (Conclusion, Rule, Explanation, Application, Conclusion), *see supra* note 6, and CRuPAC (Conclusion, Rule, Rule proof, Application, Conclusion), *see* Richard K. Neumann, Jr., *Legal Reasoning and Legal Writing* (7th ed. 2013).

It will always be articulated in general terms, and it will never include the facts of the case.

Here's an example: Assume you are researching the elements of a trade secret. Employees are prohibited from sharing information that qualifies as a trade secret. One of the elements of a trade secret is that the product cannot be "generally known" or "readily ascertainable." You uncover a case in which Holder Company claimed that DiLiuzzo disclosed a trade secret. The case examines this element. The court's holding might be expressed like this: "The Holder Company's aircraft window design was 'not generally known' and 'not readily ascertainable' because all of DiLiuzzo's efforts to reverse engineer the windows failed." Note that the holding explicitly includes the facts of the case before the court, the legal standard ("not generally known" and "not readily ascertainable") and the legal reason for the decision (all efforts to reverse engineer the product failed).

The legal principle is derived from the holding. Sometimes the court will articulate it; frequently, however, the court does not articulate it. In those situations, it is up to the reader to articulate the principle based on the court's analysis. From the above holding, a court or reader could develop the following legal principle: "A product is 'not generally known' and 'not readily ascertainable' when it cannot be reverse engineered." Note that the legal principle is phrased in general terms, and it does not include the facts of the case before the court.

Beware! Sometimes even experienced attorneys and judges mix up the holding and the legal principle. A court might state that it "holds that a product is 'not generally known' and 'not readily ascertainable' when it cannot be reverse engineered." Even though the court calls this a holding, it is not a holding; instead, it is the legal principle of the case. Likewise, a court might state that it "rules that the Holder Company's aircraft window design was 'not generally known' and 'not readily ascertainable' because all of DiLiuzzo's efforts to reverse engineer the windows failed." Just because the court used the word "rules" does not make the statement the legal principle or rule of the case; it is still the court's holding.

3. Reading

Legal reading is a learned skill; it takes a lot of time and practice to develop. Experienced legal readers usually follow a three-step process when they read a case.

Step 1: Get the Big Picture

The first step is to get the big picture of the case. This means you do the following:

- Identify the court, jurisdiction, and date. Note that all of this information is in the caption at the very top of the case.

- Get a general sense of what the case is about. Quickly reading the publisher's synopsis can be very helpful. If you don't have a synopsis to read, try reading the first sentence of every paragraph in the opinion.

- Skim the portion of the case that is relevant to your legal issue. Frequently, you can review the relevant headnotes to identify the relevant portion of the case and jump to the text of the opinion that those headnotes summarize.

Once you have the big picture, you can usually determine whether the case is relevant to your legal issue and worth closer examination.

Step 2: Read the Text Closely

- If you determine that a case is worth a closer examination, your next step is to read the text closely. The five techniques below will help you read closely.

- Read the background. Make a note of who the key parties are and what the main dispute is.

- Read the parts of the opinion that apply to your legal issue. Note that opinions usually deal with multiple legal issues, and not all of them will be relevant to your legal issue. If you're researching a trade secret issue, there's no need to read the part of the opinion that covers a tort issue. You might even draw an "x" over the paragraphs or pages that analyze irrelevant issues to save yourself time when you re-read the case. (When working online, you can highlight the irrelevant portions in red.)

- Read critically. *Critical reading* is different from passive reading, where you simply accept what is written on the page. When you read critically, you are constantly asking whether you completely understand what you just read — at a much deeper level than simply getting the general gist. Pause at the end of every paragraph or section and ask yourself if you could explain it to someone who hasn't read the case. If you can't (and frequently, the first time you read through a case, you can't), then take a moment to re-read the passage. Also, as you read critically, ask whether the court's analysis makes sense. Just because a judge wrote the opinion does not necessarily mean that the analysis is perfect. A good lawyer is able to read and explain the analysis and why it works, how it might work better, or why it doesn't work.

- Make margin notes as you read. The margin notes should include the meanings of words and phrases you had to look up.
- Label the court's analysis by issue. One of the most difficult tasks for the novice legal reader is to separate the analysis of one issue from the analysis of other issues. Labeling the parts of the court's analysis so that you can easily identify which part of the analysis goes with which issue will be very helpful. For example, assume you're reading an opinion that deals with two elements of a trade secret, the "not generally known" and "not readily ascertainable" element discussed previously, and the "efforts to maintain secrecy" element. Clearly labeling the parts of the opinion that deal with the first element will help you from conflating the analysis that the court conducts on that element from the court's analysis on the second element.

Step 3: Take Notes

The final step is to take notes on the case. Sometimes people refer to this as *briefing* the case. While there are several ways you can take notes on a case, any way you try should include the following:

- The court, parties, and year
- A very brief description of the dispute
- A brief statement of each issue
- And for each issue:
  - The law the court applied (in other words, a summary of the rule and explanation part of the opinion)
  - A summary of the court's analysis, specifically identifying the facts that triggered the court's holding
  - The holding
  - The legal principle of the case

Dividing your notes by issue will force you to keep the court's analysis of different issues separate. It will also require you to identify all of the relevant holdings and principles of the case. Novice legal readers frequently identify the holding and principle for one issue, but they then overlook the holdings and principles for the other issues in the case. Taking notes by issue will ensure that you don't miss any relevant holdings or principles. Moreover, when it's time to piece together what the law is, having case notes by issue will allow you to quickly create notes on each issue that include all of the relevant cases. You could, for example, copy and paste all of your notes for the element of efforts to maintain secrecy into one document. That way, you would have them all in one place and be better able to start determining what the law of that element is and how it might apply to your client's issue.

Appendix 10-1. Case Excerpt from the *North Western Reporter*

632   N. D.   858 NORTH WESTERN REPORTER, 2d SERIES

847 N.W.2d 761. Kovalevich's conclusory assertions about "hundreds of exhibits" was not sufficient. The court did not abuse its discretion by denying Kovalevich's motion on this issue.

C

[12] [¶ 30] Kovalevich argues the court also erred in admitting character or prior bad acts evidence under N.D.R.Ev. 404. He claims evidence, including flavored lubricant, handcuffs, and a whip, was negative character evidence which was used to prove he committed the crime. He contends the court admitted the evidence without conducting the necessary analysis required by case law and without giving a limiting instruction to the jury.

[¶ 31] Evidence of a person's character or character trait is not admissible to prove that a person acted in accordance with the character or trait on a particular occasion. N.D.R.Ev. 404(a). "Evidence of a crime, wrong, or other act is not admissible to prove a person's character in order to show that on a particular occasion the person acted in accordance with the character." N.D.R.Ev. 404(b)(1).

[¶ 32] The district court concluded N.D.R.Ev. 404 did not preclude the admission of the evidence because the victim testified the lubricant, handcuffs, and whip were with Kovalevich in Grand Forks when the crime occurred. The evidence Kovalevich argues should have been excluded is evidence of the crime and was not precluded under N.D.R.Ev. 404. The court did not abuse its discretion.

VI

[¶ 33] We conclude the district court did not err in denying Kovalevich's motion for a new trial or his motion to dismiss. We affirm the judgment.

[¶ 34] GERALD W. VANDE WALLE, C.J., DANIEL J. CROTHERS, LISA FAIR McEVERS, and CAROL RONNING KAPSNER, JJ., concur.

2015 ND 7

Robert L. JOHNSON, Petitioner
and Appellant

v.

STATE of North Dakota, Respondent
and Appellee.

No. 20140191.

Supreme Court of North Dakota.

Jan. 15, 2015.

Rehearing Denied Feb. 12, 2015.

Background: Defendant was convicted of simple assault and two counts of contact by bodily fluid or excrement. The Supreme Court reversed and remanded due to instructional error, 2001 ND 184, 636 N.W.2d 391. On remand, defendant was again convicted on the three charges. Defendant applied for postconviction relief, alleging ineffective assistance of counsel. The District Court, Stutsman County, Southeast Judicial District, John T. Paulson, J., dismissed application as untimely. Defendant appealed.

Holdings: The Supreme Court, McEvers, J., held that:

(1) trial counsel's letter acknowledging mistakes in moving for a new trial did not constitute newly-discovered evidence that would qualify defendant for an exception to the two-year deadline for filing application for postconviction relief, and

Appendix 10-1. Case Excerpt from the *North Western Reporter, continued*

JOHNSON v. STATE

Cite as 858 N.W.2d 632 (N.D. 2015)

N.D. **633**

(2) defendant waived for appellate review the issue of whether he suffered from a physical disability or mental disease that would qualify him for an exception to the two-year limitations period.

Affirmed.

1. **Criminal Law** ⟜1409, 1570

Postconviction relief proceedings are civil in nature and governed by the Rules of Civil Procedure.

2. **Criminal Law** ⟜1134.90

Supreme Court reviews an appeal from a summary denial of postconviction relief as it reviews an appeal from a summary judgment.

3. **Criminal Law** ⟜1652

The party opposing the motion for summary disposition is entitled to all reasonable inferences at the preliminary stages of a postconviction proceeding and is entitled to an evidentiary hearing if a reasonable inference raises a genuine issue of material fact.

4. **Criminal Law** ⟜1586

Trial counsel's letter acknowledging mistakes in moving for a new trial did not constitute newly-discovered evidence that would qualify defendant for an exception to the two-year deadline for filing application for postconviction relief; the letter was vague and did not include any evidentiary support of mistakes the attorney made in the motion for a new trial or accompanying brief. N.D.C.C. 29–32.1–01(3).

5. **Criminal Law** ⟜1042.7(2)

Defendant waived for appellate review the issue of whether he suffered from a physical disability or mental disease that would qualify him for an exception to the two-year deadline for filing an application for postconviction relief, where defendant failed to raise the issue in his application

or in his response to State's motion to dismiss. N.D.C.C. 29–32.1–01(3)(a)(2).

6. **Criminal Law** ⟜1028

Supreme Court will generally not address an issue on appeal not raised before the district court.

Mark T. Blumer, Fargo, ND, for petitioner and appellant; submitted on brief.

Frederick R. Fremgen (argued), Jamestown, ND, for respondent and appellee.

McEVERS, Justice.

[¶ 1] Robert L. Johnson appeals from a district court judgment summarily dismissing his application for post-conviction relief. We affirm the district court's summary dismissal of Johnson's post-conviction relief application as untimely.

I

[¶ 2] In 1999, Robert L. Johnson was charged with one count of simple assault and two counts of contact by bodily fluid or excrement. Johnson was tried and convicted of all three counts. Because of improper jury instructions, Johnson's convictions were reversed and remanded in *State v. Johnson*, 2001 ND 184, 636 N.W.2d 391. On August 16, 2002, Johnson was again convicted of all three counts. On December 11, 2002, a judgment of conviction was entered. Johnson appealed to this Court, but later withdrew his appeal after accepting a plea bargain agreement pertaining to the disposition of the appealed charges. This Court dismissed Johnson's appeal on August 13, 2003. On March 21, 2014, Johnson applied for post-conviction relief alleging ineffective assistance of counsel. In support of his application, Johnson submitted a letter dated July 17, 2013, from Johnson's 2002 trial

Chapter 11

Cases

I. Introduction

One of the most frequent sources lawyers research is case law. Chapter 10, Judicial Systems and Reading Cases, covered the North Dakota legal system and how to read a case effectively. This chapter explains how to research cases. Chapter 12, Updating, addresses how to determine whether the authorities you have found, including cases, are still "good law."

The fourth step of the research process is researching case law. There are two primary ways that researchers find cases. The first is by using topical indexes called *digests*. Digests exist both in print and online. The second is by searching the full text of judicial opinions through natural language or terms and connectors searches. This chapter will review both digests and full text searches and offer strategies to determine when to use which.

Although digests and full-text searches are the primary ways that researchers find cases, you will also find cases through secondary sources, annotated codes, and updating. How you find cases will depend on the individualized research process that you use for each research project. You will usually research cases using all or almost all of the different methods, just in different orders. It is important to master case law research using every method so that you can ensure that you have done a thorough job in every project.

II. Digests

Digests are topical indexes that researchers use to find cases. These indexes provide a straightforward and sensible way to organize cases to promote efficient researching. Here's how they work: Legal publishers, like Lexis and Westlaw, have developed extensive lists of topics that someone might want to research, like "trade secrets" or "harassment." When cases come out, the publishers analyze the opinions and index each case by topic. In other words, they identify all of the topics that a particular case addresses. Then, they list that case under each topic in an index. That way, someone researching a particular topic can easily find all of the published cases that address it by looking up the topic in the index. If you're researching trade secrets, all you would need to do to find the relevant cases that address that subject is look up the topic or topics that cover trade secrets. Publishers like Lexis and Westlaw have dedicated significant resources to creating their indexing systems, and they continue to dedicate significant resources to keeping them current. As a result, digests are powerful and efficient tools for finding case law.

A. West Digests

West digests are the most widely used digests, and they are available in print or on Westlaw. West's print digests are multi-volume sets; West's online digest is a searchable system that provides links to relevant cases. Both share the same general organization. For each topic, West provides case names and citations, along with headnotes from the cases that address the particular topic. This section of the chapter describes the features of the West digests and explains how to use the West digests in print and online.

1. Organization

West's digests are organized by *topics* and *key numbers*. First, *topics* are broad legal subjects, like Assault and Battery, Civil Rights, and Property. West currently has over 425 topics in its digest system. Each print digest has an alphabetical numbered list of topics at the very beginning; the same list is available on Westlaw's Key Numbers link in the "All Content" tab, and also on the West Key Number System in the "Tools" tab. See Figure 11-1 for an excerpt of the topic list that appears for Westlaw's Key Numbers.

Each topic is further divided into narrower sub-topics. These sub-topics are represented by *key numbers*. To research whether your client could claim self-defense as a defense to battery, you would first look for the most relevant topic, Assault and Battery, as shown in Figure 11-1. Then, you would drill down into the sub-topics to find more specifically what you were looking for. As shown in Figure 11-2, there is a key number that corresponds with self-defense as a defense to assault and battery, and there are North Dakota cases on point.

You can also see that, once you have located the relevant key number, West provides the case name, citation, and headnote relevant to your topic. Reviewing the headnotes can be a quick way to determine whether a case is going to be helpful or not.

Figure 11-1. Key Numbers on Westlaw

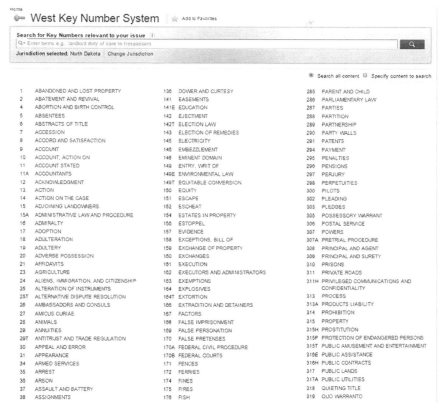

Source: Westlaw. Reprinted with permission of Thomson Reuters.

2. Using West's Print Digests

a. The Process

Step 1: Select the Appropriate Digest

The volumes within print digests are arranged much like an encyclopedia, alphabetically with words on the spine to tell you what range of topics are covered inside. West has print digest sets for almost every state, including North Dakota. West has sets for each geographical reporter series as well, so you can also find North Dakota cases in the *North Western Digest*. In addition to the geographical sets, West has sets for certain courts, including the U.S. Supreme Court, the bankruptcy court, the federal claims court, and military courts.

Figure 11-2. Key Numbers Under Assault and Battery

Clicking on Assault and Battery takes you to an outline of sub-topics. From there, drill down to find the key number that addresses self-defense.

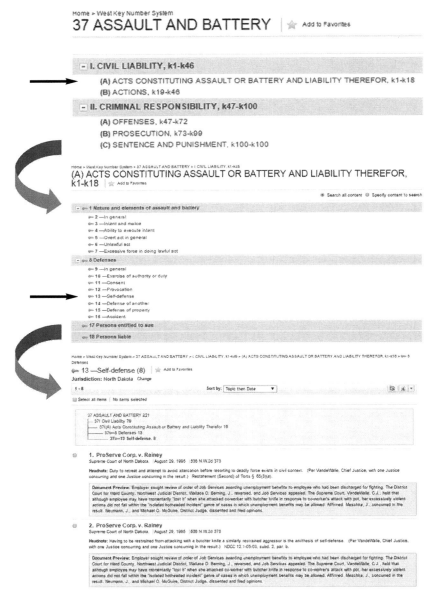

The *Federal Practice Digest* includes headnotes from decisions from U.S. district and appellate courts.

Step 2: Identify and Locate Relevant Topics and Key Numbers

Once you have selected the appropriate digest set to use, your next task is to locate the topic that covers your issue. If you already know the topic that addresses your issue, then you can simply find the right volume by looking at the spines and locating the one with your topic. For example, if you know that Assault and Battery is a topic, you can go directly to the volume that has it.

If you aren't sure which topic addresses your issue, you can look at the Descriptive-Word Index. Each set of print digest volumes has its own Descriptive-Word Index. In it, you can look up your search terms and find potentially relevant topics and key numbers, which you can then locate in the digest volumes. If you did not already know that Assault and Battery was a topic, you could look up "battery" in the Descriptive-Word Index. It would direct you to the topic Assault and Battery, along with several relevant sub-topics, represented by key numbers.

You're not finished with the Descriptive-Word Index yet. The Descriptive-Word Index is current only as of the copyright date of the digest volume. Between publications, the index stays current through the use of pocket parts. Check the back cover of the Descriptive-Word Index for the pocket part, look for your search terms there, and make a note of any additional topics and key numbers you find.

Step 3: Look Up the Relevant Topics and Key Numbers

Once you have identified and located the volume (or volumes) housing the relevant topics and key numbers, your next step is to look them up. Each volume is arranged alphabetically. When you turn to your topic, you will find a brief outline of the sub-topics covered. After that outline, you will find citations to relevant cases and the relevant headnote or headnotes from those cases.

Read the headnotes carefully to determine which cases are relevant to your search. Sometimes a significant number of headnotes will appear under a particular sub-topic. Resist the temptation to skim through the headnotes quickly because the risk of bypassing a relevant case is too high. Likewise, resist the temptation to just jot down every case listed to look up. A careful review of the headnotes is the only way to conduct both thorough and efficient research.

As with the Descriptive-Word Index, the digest volumes are current only through the copyright date. As a result, you will need to check the pocket part in the back cover of the digest for headnotes for the most recent cases. If the pocket part becomes too big to put in the back cover of the digest, the publisher will provide a paperback supplementary volume of updated material. That will be shelved next to the volume it supplements. These paperback supplementary volumes are then updated with *cumulative supplementary pamphlets*. These pamphlets contain supplements for all of the paperback supplementary volumes, so they are usually shelved after all of the volumes in the digest. The cover will show the publication date of the pamphlet, as well as the dates of the pocket parts it updates.

b. Other Features of the Print Digest
i. Words and Phrases

While you can look up general definitions of words and phrases in *Black's Law Dictionary*, sometimes words and phrases have special judge-made definitions in particular jurisdictions. Judicial definitions are particularly helpful when an important word in a statute is vague or ambiguous. You can find cases that define certain words and phrases in the Words and Phrases volumes. The Words and Phrases volumes are at the end of the digest volumes. At the end of each case entry, you will see the topics and key numbers that apply to that case's headnotes.

Note, the Words and Phrases volumes are different from the main digest volumes: The Words and Phrases volumes focus very narrowly on cases that specifically define certain words and phrases; the main volume will direct you to a broader body of cases, some of which specifically define certain words and phrases, but some of which only discuss or explain them.

As with the other volumes in the print digests, the Words and Phrases volumes are updated with pocket parts.

ii. Table of Cases

If you know one or both parties' names in a case but don't know the citation, you can find it in the Table of Cases. The Table of Cases lists all cases indexed in a digest series by the primary plaintiff's name and the primary defendant's name. The Table provides the full name of the case, the citation, and the relevant topics and key numbers. As with the other volumes in the print digests, the Table of Cases is updated with pocket parts.

3. Using West's Digests Online

As noted above, Westlaw's Key Numbers System is the online version of the West digest. You can access the Key Numbers System through a link in either

Figure 11-3. Word Searching Key Numbers

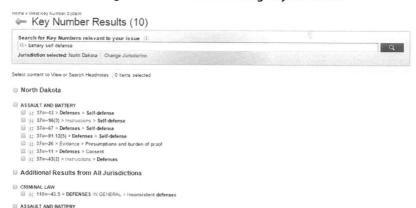

Source: Westlaw. Reprinted with permission of Thomson Reuters.

the "All Content" tab or the "Tools" tab. The first page of the Key Numbers System is the list of topics. From here, there are several ways to access topics and key numbers.

Using the Outline. One way to search topics and key numbers is to use the outline. Click the topic that you want to explore, and you can drill down into that topic until you find the sub-topics you are looking for. You'll see that, in addition to headnotes, the online digest also includes a "Document Preview" in which you can read a short description of the case.

Word Searching Key Numbers. Another way to search is to conduct a full-text search directly for key numbers related to your issue. Use the key number search box and type in your terms. You can use either natural language or terms and connectors searching. Westlaw will identify key numbers with your terms. See Figure 11-3.

Word Searching Headnotes. You can also search headnotes directly with your terms, using either natural language or terms and connectors searching. Westlaw will identify headnotes with your search terms and the key numbers that go with those headnotes. See Figure 11-4.

Searching from a Relevant Case. Finally, if you have a relevant case, you can access the digest system through that case. To do so, find the relevant head-

Figure 11-4. Word Searching Headnotes

Input your search terms into the headnote search box.

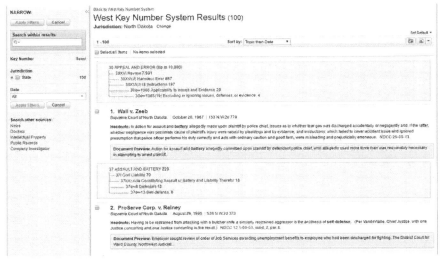

Source: Westlaw. Reprinted with permission of Thomson Reuters.

note and click on the key number sub-topic. When you do, Westlaw will take you to the cases and headnotes for that sub-topic. See Figure 11-5.

B. Lexis Topics and Headnotes

Like Westlaw, Lexis has developed its own system of topics and headnotes. Notably, Lexis's and Westlaw's topics and headnotes do not correspond with each other. Therefore, a topic in Westlaw is not going to be the same as a topic in Lexis, and the headnotes in each will likely be similar, but they will not be identical.

To access the Lexis topics and headnotes system, click on "Browse" and select "Topics." You can then either do a word search for topics or drill down from there. See Figure 11-6.

You can also access the Lexis topics and headnotes system through a case. To do so, locate the relevant headnote. After the headnote, you will see all of the topics and sub-topics that apply to that headnote. Click on one of the topics or sub-topics to either get all documents with headnotes in the same

Figure 11-5. Accessing the Digest from a Case

First, find the relevant headnote and click on the key number sub-topic.

Then, Westlaw will take you to the cases and headnotes for that sub-topic.

Figure 11-6. Using Topics and Headnotes on Lexis

Select "Browse," then "Topics," and either word search in the text box or continue clicking through to drill down.

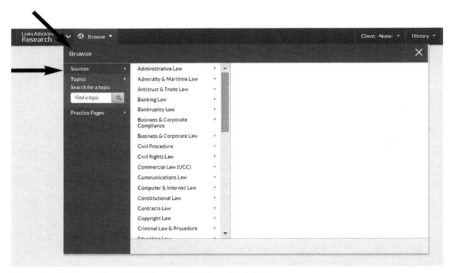

Source: Lexis Advance. Reprinted with permission from Reed Elsevier.

category, or you can view that topic or sub-topic in the index and navigate from there. You can also set an alert for Lexis to update you when new cases in the same category come out. See Figure 11-7.

III. Using Text Searches to Find Cases Online

In addition to Westlaw's online digest and Lexis's topics and headnotes system, you can find cases online through text searching. There are two steps to the process of finding cases through text searching, as explained in Chapter 2, Research Techniques.

Step 1: Select Your Database

The first step is to select your database. You can think of this step as selecting the world of cases that you want the service to search.

The most common selection you will make is the jurisdiction or jurisdictions you want to search. In both Lexis and Westlaw, you can select your jurisdiction through the top search box. Note that you can select geographical jurisdictions,

Figure 11-7. Find the Relevant Headnote and Link to the Topic System

Find the relevant headnote and click on the relevant topic or sub-topic and select the appropriate action from the pop-up menu.

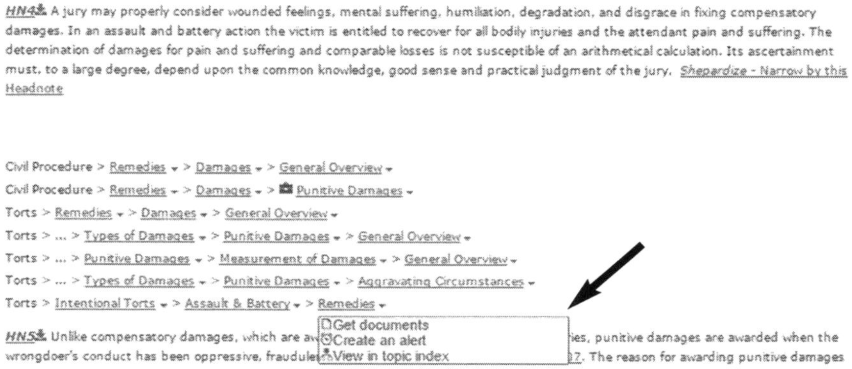

HN4 A jury may properly consider wounded feelings, mental suffering, humiliation, degradation, and disgrace in fixing compensatory damages. In an assault and battery action the victim is entitled to recover for all bodily injuries and the attendant pain and suffering. The determination of damages for pain and suffering and comparable losses is not susceptible of an arithmetical calculation. Its ascertainment must, to a large degree, depend upon the common knowledge, good sense and practical judgment of the jury. *Shepardize - Narrow by this Headnote*

Civil Procedure > Remedies ▾ > Damages ▾ > General Overview ▾
Civil Procedure > Remedies ▾ > Damages ▾ > 🖴 Punitive Damages ▾
Torts > Remedies ▾ > Damages ▾ > General Overview ▾
Torts > ... > Types of Damages ▾ > Punitive Damages ▾ > General Overview ▾
Torts > ... > Punitive Damages ▾ > Measurement of Damages ▾ > General Overview ▾
Torts > ... > Types of Damages ▾ > Punitive Damages ▾ > Aggravating Circumstances ▾
Torts > Intentional Torts ▾ > Assault & Battery ▾ > Remedies ▾

☐ Get documents
⊗ Create an alert
👁 View in topic index

HN5 Unlike compensatory damages, which are a... ies, punitive damages are awarded when the wrongdoer's conduct has been oppressive, fraudule... 7. The reason for awarding punitive damages

Source: Lexis Advance. Reprinted with permission from Reed Elsevier.

like North Dakota or the Eighth Circuit, or you can select particular courts, like the North Dakota Supreme Court or the tax court. See Figures 2-1 in Chapter 2 for an example of how to select jurisdiction on Lexis, and see 11-8 below for an example on Westlaw.

Other selections might include area of law. You can select for area of law on Lexis through the top search box and narrow by "Practice Area and Topic." See Figure 11-9. You can select for area of law on Westlaw by clicking on the "Practice Area" tab visible on the home page.

Step 2: Input Your Search

Once you have selected the world of cases to search, you can input your search terms into the top search box. You can use either natural language or terms and connectors. As noted in Chapter 2, Research Techniques, it is usually helpful to start with natural language and follow up with terms and connectors to ensure that you have collected all relevant results.

IV. Which Should You Use: Digests v. Text Searching

Novice researchers frequently default to text searching because it is more familiar to them. This is a mistake. As a general rule, digests are the most ef-

Figure 11-8. Selecting Jurisdiction on Westlaw

Source: Westlaw. Reprinted with permission of Thomson Reuters.

ficient and effective way to identify relevant and important cases. If you conduct your research using only digests, you will almost certainly uncover every case that you need. This does not mean that text searching is unimportant. Indeed, the most thorough approach is to use both digests and text searches. And sometimes it makes sense to start with text searching. Here are tips on when to start with digests and when to start with text searching.

Starting with a digest is likely the most effective approach when you are looking for specific information in a specific area of law. So, if you want to know the definition of a trade secret in North Dakota law, the digests should be your first stop. After you have completed your digest search, you should consider following it up with a text search. The text search serves two purposes: First, the text search allows you to ensure that your digest search was complete. Sometimes, particularly in new areas of law, you might overlook a relevant topic in the digests. A quick text search will alert you to whether there is a body of cases that you have overlooked. Second, the text search allows you to pull opinions that have not been indexed by Lexis or Westlaw. Unpublished opinions have frequently not been indexed. While they are of less precedential value than published opinions, they may contain helpful analysis or present a fact pattern more analogous to your client's than the published opinions.

Figure 11-9. Selecting Area of Law on Lexis

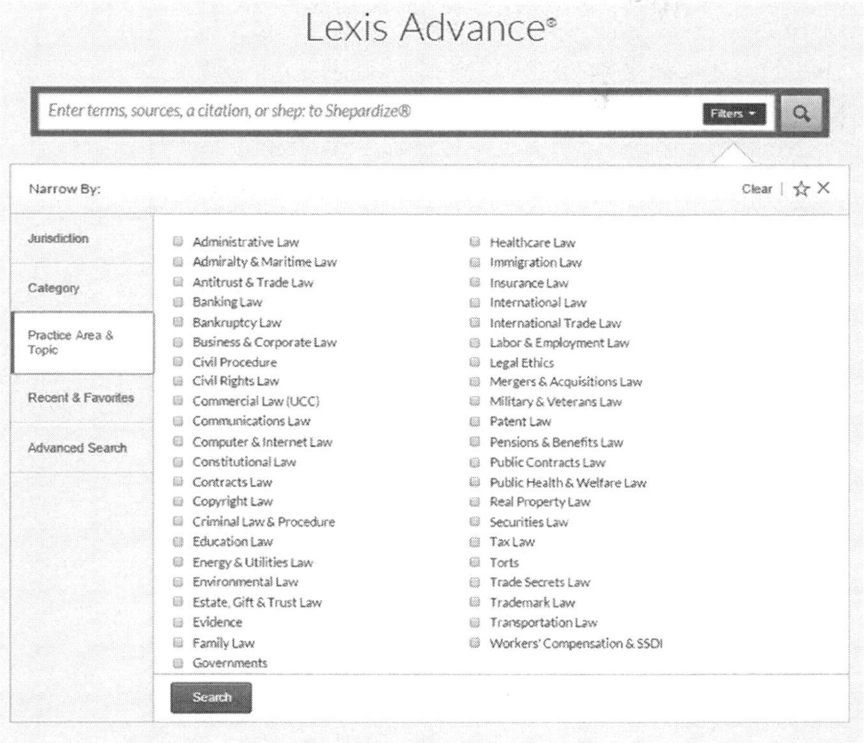

Source: Lexis Advance. Reprinted with permission from Reed Elsevier.

However, when you really don't know what you are looking for, text searching might be the best starting place. You won't always know what you are looking for; a client won't come through the door announcing that she has a trade secret claim. Instead, she'll have a story. You might immediately recognize the legal issues in her story, but you might not. When you don't, putting some search terms you have generated from her story into a text search might help you uncover potential legal issues.

Text searching might also be the best starting place when you know what you are looking for, but it just doesn't exist. You won't always find what you are looking for: Sometimes, you'll face an issue of first impression. This happens more frequently in smaller states with smaller bodies of law, like North Dakota. When this happens, it might be helpful to find analogous legal issues. For example, you might have a seventeen-year-old client who wants to make her own medical decisions. You know that the mature minor doctrine would allow her to do so, but the North Dakota courts haven't yet encountered a mature minor doctrine case. As a result, researching "mature minor doctrine" in North Dakota is not going to produce results. You might, however, find analogous cases and bodies of law if you searched for your terms more broadly.

Once your text searches have helped you narrow down what issues you're researching or what bodies of law might be fruitful, you will probably want to switch over to digest searching. At that point, the digests will be both efficient and effective. After you have completed your digest searching, you might still want to follow up with a few quick text searches to ensure that you found everything you need.

Chapter 12

Updating

I. Introduction

The last several chapters covered researching enacted law and case law. In researching the law, you always need to ensure that you are using law that is still valid. This chapter explains how to do that.

A *citator* is an index of authorities that cite a particular legal authority. Legal researchers use citators for two reasons: First, researchers use citators to ensure that the authority they are using is still valid, or "good law." Second, researchers use citators to expand their research by finding authorities that rely on and sometimes discuss the authority they are researching. Together, these two functions are referred to as *updating*. You might also hear senior attorneys call this process *Sheparding* because the first resource to collect and index citations in a citator was the print series *Shepard's Citations*.

II. Checking the Validity of Authorities

The law is ever-changing; one of your most important responsibilities as a researcher is to be aware of the status of every authority on which you rely. Therefore, one of the steps of the research process is determining whether the authorities you find are still good law. To do this, you'll need to find out whether a court or legislature has overturned or modified your authorities. After you have determined whether your authorities are still good law, your job is not yet complete. You must then find and be aware of any *adverse authority*, which includes authorities that question, disagree with, or distinguish the authority you're researching.

Ultimately, ensuring that you're relying on valid law and that you're aware of adverse authority will save you from embarrassment. More importantly, it is an ethical obligation: Courts expect attorneys to cite valid law and any adverse authority that questions or disagrees with the cited law.

A. The Basic Process

The process for using citators is fairly simple; the analysis of what you find is both difficult and time consuming. In a nutshell, you will look up the citation of the authority you're using in a citator. The citation you're looking up is usually referred to as the *cited source*. You'll then see a symbol which will tell you whether the cited source is still valid, valid but with some adverse authority, or overturned.

The citator will list all of the authorities that have relied on the cited source. The authorities that have relied on the cited source are referred to as the *citing sources*, or sometimes *citing references* or *citing decisions*. The citing sources can include adverse authority, authorities that include positive discussions about the cited source, or just authorities that cite to the cited source for a minor proposition of law.

One of your jobs will be to determine what to review. You will not always have the luxury of time to be able to review all citing sources. When you're pressed for time, you should always review any adverse authority to figure out what it means. Significantly, just because a cited source appears to have been overturned does not mean that it is bad law for all issues. For example, a cited source might have the overturned symbol next to it but still be good law for the point you're researching. The citing source that overturned the cited source might have overturned the holding on only one issue out of the many that the case addressed. That means that parts of the cited source are still good law.

Reviewing all adverse authority will help you figure out which parts of the cited source are still good law. After you have reviewed all adverse authority, you should review all citing sources from your jurisdiction that have addressed the citing source. If time permits, you can review the remaining sources. As you will see below, you can narrow your list of citing sources by certain metrics. Doing so will help you prioritize what to review.

Finally, remember that many research projects will take more than just one day. Therefore, updating is not something you do just once. Instead, updating is a continuous process. You should always update as you conduct your research and again before you submit a document to a supervisor or appear before a court. If your project is one that spans a long period of time, you should update periodically to be sure you don't spend a significant amount of time relying on a source only to discover that is was overturned sometime after you first discovered it.

The two most common citators are Shepard's on Lexis and KeyCite on Westlaw, and this chapter explains the mechanics of using both. You should know

Figure 12-1. Accessing Shepard's When You Know the Citation

Type shep:, then the citation, check your jurisdiction, and hit enter on your keyboard or click the search icon.

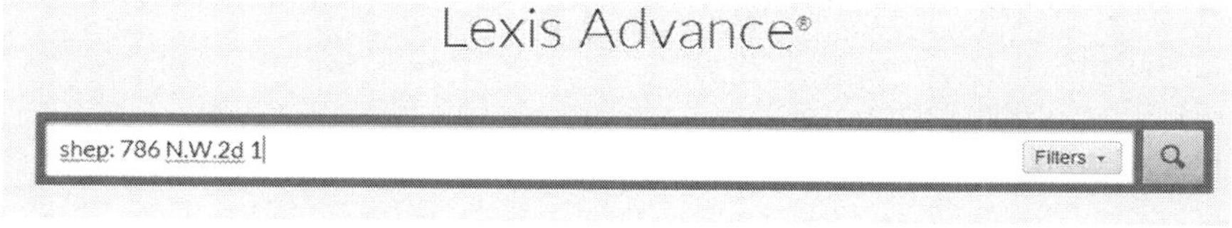

Source: Lexis Advance. Reprinted with permission from Reed Elsevier.

that the coverage of both services is extensive, but not identical. Moreover, they use different symbols to illustrate the relationship between cited sources and citing sources.

B. Shepard's on Lexis

1. Where to Find Shepard's

You can access Shepard's from two places on Lexis.

First, if you know the citation of the authority you're checking, you can simply go to the main search box at the top of the page, type shep: followed by the citation. Check to be sure that your filter is set to either "filter" or the appropriate jurisdiction, and hit enter. See Figure 12-1.

Second, if you're already looking at an authority in Lexis, you can click the "Shepardize this document" link on the right-hand side of the page. Alternatively, you can click on the Shepard's symbol that appears next to the authority's name in the center of the page. See Figure 12-2.

2. How to Use Shepard's

a. The Shepard's Signals

Shepard's uses different symbols to communicate the status of the document. For a case, a red stop sign indicates strong negative analysis of the cited source; a circle with a red exclamation point means the same for a statute. A yellow square with a "Q" means that there is analysis questioning the cited source. A yellow triangle indicates possible negative analysis impacting the cited source. A yellow, upside-down triangle with an exclamation point means that there is pending legislation that affects the cited source. A summary of selected symbols and what they mean appears in Table 12-1.

Figure 12-2. Accessing Shepard's from a Document

Click "Shepardize this document" or click on the Shepard's symbol next to the cited source's name.

Source: Lexis Advance. Reprinted with permission from Reed Elsevier.

b. The Shepard's User Interface

Shepard's displays citing sources on a few different pages. For cases, the first is Appellate Decisions; the second is Citing Decisions. For statutes, the first is Citing Decisions; the second is Other Citing Sources. All of these pages are discussed more fully below. Initially accessing Shepard's for a case will take you directly to the Appellate Decisions page. You can access the other pages through a list of tabs to the left of the screen. See Figure 12-3. Once you have accessed Shepard's for a statute, it will take you directly to the Citing Decisions page. Note that, at the top of the page, Lexis will notify you whether pending legislation affects the cited statute. If there is adverse authority for the cited source, a red stop sign will appear next to the appropriate tab, as shown previously in Figure 12-2.

The Appellate Decisions tab appears only for cases. On the Appellate Decisions page, you can see direct and indirect appellate history for the cited source. For example, if the cited source was a case that was subsequently appealed and reversed, this information will appear on the Appellate Decisions page.

The Citing Decisions page shows all of the cases and administrative decisions that have cited your source. One of the things you can learn from the Citing Decisions page is whether any of the sources have called your source into question. The symbol next to "Cited by" shows the treatment your citation received in the listed authority. *Treatment* refers to how a citing source evaluated the

Table 12-1. Shepard's Signals

Symbol	Meaning for Cases	Meaning for Statutes
(stop sign)	Warning: There is strong negative analysis impacting the case.	N/A
(exclamation)	N/A	Warning: There is strong negative analysis impacting this statute.
Q	There is analysis questioning the precedential value of the case.	N/A
(triangle)	There is possible negative analysis impacting the case.	N/A
(plus diamond)	The case has been followed by other cases.	N/A
A	Neutral analysis is available for the case.	N/A
I	There are citing references available that do not include analysis.	N/A

cited source. For example, negative treatment might mean that the citing source questioned the cited source; positive treatment might mean that the citing source agreed with the cited source. The Citing Decisions page is useful not only for checking whether the cited source is still valid, but also for expanding your research, discussed further later in this chapter.

On the Table of Authorities page, you can see a list of all of the authorities your cited source relied on and their Shepard's signals. While the Table of Authorities does not reveal to you how subsequent courts and legislatures have treated your authority, it will help you determine whether the law on which your citation relied is good law. Reviewing the Table of Authorities will help you conduct your own independent analysis of whether your authority is likely good law.

Figure 12-3. Shepard's Tabs for Cases

Source: Lexis Advance. Reprinted with permission from Reed Elsevier.

The Other Citing Sources page lists all secondary sources and other statutes that have referred to the cited source. While the Other Citing Sources page won't tell you whether the cited source is still good law, it is very helpful in expanding your research.

c. Understanding and Accessing Citing Sources on Shepard's

Before each citing source, Lexis includes, in bold, terms that explain how the cited source is treated by the citing source. These might include "Followed by," "Explained by," and "Cited by." These terms will give you a sense of how deeply each citing source treats the cited source. See Figure 12-4.

To access a citing source, all you need to do is click on the case name. Lexis will take you directly to the portion of the citing source that addresses the cited source. Note that you can also access the Shepard's results for each of your citing sources. You'll see a Shepard's symbol next to each citing source. To access the Shepard's results for the citing source, just click on the Shepard's symbol next to the name of the source. (And be sure not to conflate the symbol for the citing source with the symbol for the cited source!) See Figure 12-4.

d. Limiting Shepard's Search Results

Sometimes, you'll look up a source with dozens or even hundreds of citing sources. You won't be able to read each source in these circumstances, so you'll need to limit the search results to only those that are the most relevant. Shepard's lets you do that. To the left of the Shepard's page is a column that lets you narrow your list by certain metrics. You can filter by treatment analysis

Figure 12-4. Understanding and Accessing Sources on Shepard's

The arrows indicate treatment terms and the Shepard's signal for each citing source.

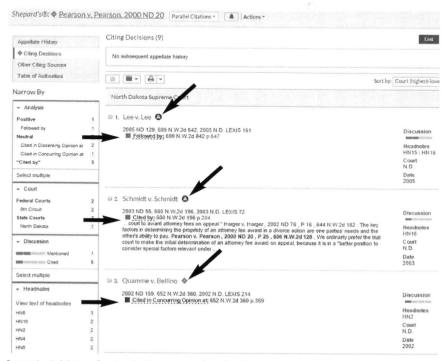

Source: Lexis Advance. Reprinted with permission from Reed Elsevier.

(negative, positive, or other), jurisdiction, headnotes, dates, and terms. If your goal is to determine whether your source is still good law, you should narrow by analysis. The most relevant to this determination will be "warning," which means that the authority has been overturned at least in part, and "caution," which means that the authority has been distinguished or called into question.

C. KeyCite on Westlaw

1. Where to Find KeyCite

You can access KeyCite from two places on Westlaw.

First, if you know the citation of the authority you're checking, you can simply go to the main search box at the top of the page, type keycite or kc, fol-

Figure 12-5. Accessing KeyCite with a Citation

Type keycite or kc, then the citation, check your jurisdiction, and hit enter on your keyboard or click the search icon.

Source: Westlaw. Reprinted with permission of Thomson Reuters.

lowed by the citation, and check to be sure that your jurisdiction is set to the appropriate place. Either hit enter or click the search button. See Figure 12-5.

Second, if you're already looking at an authority in Westlaw, you can click one of the tabs towards the top of the page. Alternatively, you can click on the KeyCite symbol that appears next to the authority's name in the upper left-hand corner of the page. See Figure 12-6.

2. How to Use KeyCite

a. The KeyCite Symbols

KeyCite uses different symbols to communicate the status of a cited source. When the citation has negative history, either a red or yellow flag appears next to the case name. A red flag means that the cited source is not valid for at least one point of law. But recall that it may still be good law in many other respects. A yellow flag means that the cited source is valid authority, but it has been

Figure 12-6. Accessing KeyCite from the Authority

Click the Negative Treatment tab or either of the KeyCite symbols. Doing so will take you directly to the Negative Treatment page.

Source: Westlaw. Reprinted with permission of Thomson Reuters.

Table 12-2. KeyCite Symbols

Symbol	Meaning for cases	Meaning for statute
Red flag	The case is no longer good for at least one point of law.	The statute has been amended, repealed, superseded, or held unconstitutional in whole or in part.
Yellow flag	The case has some negative history, but it has not been overruled.	Typically means that the statute has some negative history, such as a case calling it into doubt, but it has not been overruled.
Blue and white flag	The case is on appeal to a U.S. Court of Appeals or the U.S. Supreme Court.	N/A
Green quotation marks	The citing source directly quotes the cited case.	N/A

called into some question. A summary of selected symbols and what they mean appears in Table 12-2.

b. The KeyCite User Interface

When you're viewing an authority on Westlaw, the KeyCite interface appears at the top of the page through a series of tabs, including Negative Treatment, History, Citing References, and Table of Authorities. See Figure 12-7.

The first relevant tab is labeled Negative Treatment. If you click on that tab, a page with both negative direct history and all of the adverse authorities for the cited source will appear. KeyCite will identify which treated the cited source most negatively, which can help you prioritize your reading. See Figure 12-7.

A cited source might have no negative history. If the cited source has no negative history, then there will be no flag or other symbol next to the source name. Additionally, the Negative Treatment tab will be more lightly colored than the other tabs, and when you click on it, nothing will happen.

The next relevant tab is the History tab. By clicking on it, you can access the direct history of the cited source. As a result, you will be able to see available opinions from previous or subsequent proceedings in the case. See Figure 12-8.

A cited source may have no history, or its history may not be accessible on Westlaw. In that situation, the History tab will be more lightly colored than the other tabs, and will not lead anywhere when you click on it.

Figure 12-7. Accessing KeyCite from the Authority

Here is what the Negative Treatment page looks like:

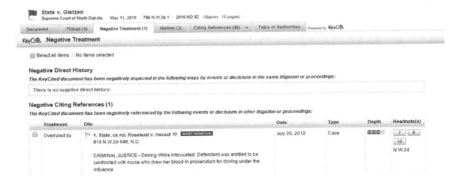

Source: Westlaw. Reprinted with permission of Thomson Reuters.

Figure 12-8. KeyCite History

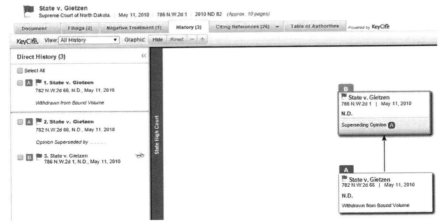

Source: Westlaw. Reprinted with permission of Thomson Reuters.

The next relevant tab is Citing References. On the Citing References page, you can see all of the cases, secondary sources, and appellate briefs that have cited your case. This page shows the treatment each source gave the cited source, along with the depth of that treatment and the headnote to which the discussion pertains. This page is useful not only for checking whether the cited source is still valid, but also for expanding your research. See Figure 12-9.

Figure 12-9. KeyCite Citing References

State v. Gietzen
Supreme Court of North Dakota.   May 11, 2010   786 N.W.2d 1   2010 ND 82   (Approx. 10 pages)

Document | Filings (2) | Negative Treatment (1) | History (3) | **Citing References (26)** ▼ | Table of Authorities   *Powered by* KeyCite

KeyCite **Citing References (26)**   1-26   Sort By: Depth: Highest First ▼

VIEW:
Cases — 6
Secondary Sources — 14
Appellate Court Documents — 6
All Results — 26

NARROW:
Apply Filters | Cancel
Search within results
Choose a content type under "VIEW" to see filtering options

No items selected

Treatment	Title	Date	Type	Depth	Headnote(s)
Overruled by [NEGATIVE]	1. State, ex rel. Roseland v. Herauf 〃 819 N.W.2d 546, 553+, N.D. CRIMINAL JUSTICE - Driving While Intoxicated. Defendant was entitled to be confronted with nurse who drew her blood in prosecution for driving under the influence.	July 26, 2012	Case	▮▮▮	7 9 10 N.W.2d
Discussed by	2. Brief of Appellee 〃 THE STATE OF NORTH DAKOTA, Plaintiff and Appellee, v. Brett Evan SAUER, Defendant and Appellant. 2010 WL 5382255, *5382255+, N.D. (Appellate Brief)	Nov 2010	Brief	▮▮▮	7 9 10 N.W.2d
Cited by	3. State ex rel. Madden v. Rustad 〃 823 N.W.2d 767, 768+, N.D. CRIMINAL JUSTICE - Evidence. State was not required to produce director of crime lab to testify about analytical report for which director had no involvement in preparing.	Nov. 27, 2012	Case	▮▮▮	7 9 10 N.W.2d
Cited by	4. State v. Lutz 〃 820 N.W.2d 111, 116, N.D. CRIMINAL JUSTICE - Confrontation. State was required to produce at trial nurse who drew DUI defendant's blood sample.	July 26, 2012	Case	▮▮▮	7 9 10 N.W.2d
Cited by	5. Derr v. State 〃 29 A.3d 533, 561+, Md. CRIMINAL JUSTICE - Confrontation. Rule allowing expert to base opinion on inadmissible evidence violates Confrontation Clause when inadmissible evidence consists of testimonial...	Sep. 29, 2011	Case	▮▮▮	10 N.W.2d

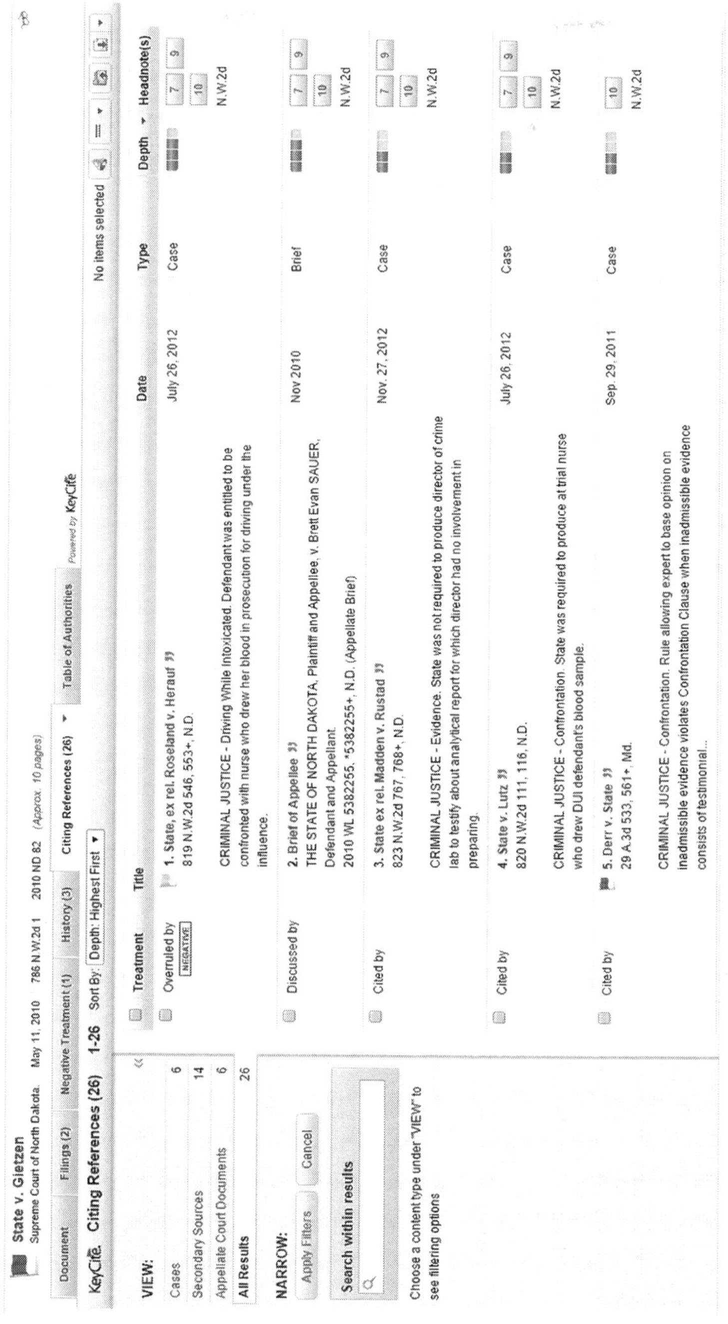

Source: Westlaw. Reprinted with permission of Thomson Reuters.

The final tab is the Table of Authorities tab, which leads to a list of all of the authorities your citation relied on and their KeyCite signals. As noted above, the Table of Authorities does not reveal to you how subsequent courts and legislatures have treated your authority. But it will help you determine whether the law on which your citation relied is good law. Reviewing the Table of Authorities can help you as you conduct your own independent analysis of whether the cited source is likely good law.

c. Understanding and Accessing Citing Sources on KeyCite

Before each citing source, Westlaw includes terms that explain how the cited source is treated by the citing source. These might include "Cited by" and "Mentioned by." Westlaw will also tell you whether that treatment was negative. Together, these two pieces of information will give you a sense of how each citing source treats the cited source. Westlaw will also show you how much the citing source discussed the cited source. This is called "depth of treatment," and Westlaw depicts it by showing four squares. The number of squares shaded green indicates the depth of treatment. So, one green square out of four probably means that the citing source only cited the cited source; four green squares likely means that there was an extensive discussion of the cited source. Refer to Figure 12-9 to see these features.

You can access a citing source by clicking on the case name. Westlaw will take you directly to the portion of the citing source that addresses the cited source. Note that you can also access the KeyCite results for each of your citing sources by clicking the KeyCite symbol next to the name of each citing source. (And, again, you must not confuse the symbol for the citing source with the symbol for the cited source!)

d. Limiting KeyCite Search Results

When a cited source has dozens or even hundreds of citing sources, you'll have to prioritize which you read. To limit the search results to only those that are the most relevant, look on the left side of the page for a column where you can select a type of document to view. Select a type of document, like cases, and a list of metrics appears below that you can use to filter your results. You can filter by treatment status (e.g., view or hide negative), jurisdiction, headnotes, and depth of treatment. To determine whether your source is still good law, narrow by treatment status to view sources that give negative treatment.

III. Using Citators to Expand Your Research

In addition to helping you determine whether a cited source is still good law, Shepard's and KeyCite are also useful tools for expanding your research. Once you have found a highly relevant source, chances are that some of its citing sources are relevant, too. Moreover, when the cited source is a case, subsequent cases may explain the cited source in a way that might help you better understand its analysis. Similarly, when the cited source is a statute, subsequent cases might provide helpful analysis of the statute or allow you to see the statute applied in context. Ultimately, updating is a powerful research tool for evaluating sources you find and for helping you find more sources like them.

Chapter 13

Ballot Measures

I. Introduction

In North Dakota, ballot measures are an important source of law and researching them should be part of your research strategy, along with reviewing secondary sources, researching the major sources of primary law, and ensuring that your research is up-to-date.

Ballot measures are proposed statutory laws or constitutional amendments, or proposals to repeal previously passed laws, that are placed on a ballot for direct vote by the electorate. They represent a form of "direct democracy"—that is, instead of the law being passed or repealed solely through the ordinary legislative, judicial, or administrative rulemaking process, the people become directly involved, casting votes on the particular measure in question.

There are multiple types of ballot measures. The most common type is a "legislative measure," also sometimes called a "legislative referendum" or "referred measure." These are measures that the legislature opts to put on the ballot for popular vote. All states allow these types of measures, and all but Delaware actually require them for proposed constitutional amendments.

Some states, including North Dakota, also allow other types of ballot measures that are even more directly democratic, enlisting the voters not just in deciding whether a law should be adopted or rejected but also allowing the voters themselves to place measures on the ballot. These ballot measures are called "initiatives" or "referendums."

Initiatives are laws or constitutional amendments that are proposed by the citizens. *Referendums* (also sometimes called "popular referendums" to avoid confusion with legislative referendums) are proposals by the citizens to reject a law that has already been passed. Initiatives and referendums are placed on the ballot via a citizen petition process that varies from state to state. The process in North Dakota is explained in more detail in Part II.B. of this chapter.

Not all states allow citizen initiatives and referendums, and of those that do, some still require some form of legislative approval; in other words, the legislature must still approve the measure before it will be placed on the ballot. States that require this kind of legislative approval are said to have an "indirect" initiative or referendum process. North Dakota is one of a handful of states that allow both direct initiatives and direct referendums. This means that, assuming all of the petition requirements are met, citizens can essentially bypass the state legislature and put measures directly on the ballot.

II. Initiatives and Referendums in North Dakota

A. Overview

Citizen-driven initiatives and referendums have a long and important history in North Dakota. After several years of public agitation, a state constitutional amendment was passed in 1914 that created the initiative and referendum process in the state. Four years later, the first seven initiatives appeared as proposed constitutional amendments on the 1918 ballot.[1]

Although in recent times changes in state law have made the initiative and referendum process slightly more difficult to navigate, citizen-driven lawmaking is still important in North Dakota, and the state has consistently ranked as one of the top five states in the number of initiatives.[2] In fact, during the 2014 elections, four initiatives appeared on the ballot (as well as five legislatively referred constitutional amendments). Given this history, North Dakota legal researchers must understand how the initiative and referendum process works.

B. The Initiative and Referendum Process

The initiative and referendum process in North Dakota is governed by Article III of the North Dakota Constitution[3] as well as several state statutes.[4] These laws address such matters as petition signature requirements, deadlines, and the provision of a fiscal impact statement.

---

1. All seven passed, including an amendment that allowed for the creation of the Bank of North Dakota, which is still the only state-run bank in the nation.
2. *See* http://www.iandrinstitute.org/North%20Dakota.htm.
3. N.D. Const. art. III, §§ 1-9.
4. *See* N.D. Cent. Code § 16.1-01-01(2)(e); §§ 16.1-01-09 to -11; and § 16.1-06-09.

Citizens who want to initiate or refer laws must first draft a petition and submit it to the Secretary of State. The Secretary of State will create a title for the measure and ensure that the format is correct. Each petition must be sponsored by at least twenty-five qualified North Dakota voters, who act as the sponsoring committee.

After the Secretary of State approves the petition, the sponsoring committee can commence obtaining the required number of voter signatures. Under Article III, for constitutional amendments, a petition must be signed by at least 4% of the state population. For other initiatives or for referendums, the petition must be signed by at least 2% of the state population.

Once the sponsoring committee has obtained the required number of signatures, the petition must again be submitted to the Secretary of State for final approval. For initiatives, the sponsoring committee has a year from the date the original petition is approved to submit the signatures. For referendums, the signatures must be submitted within ninety days of when the law being referred was enacted. In either case, the petition must be filed with the Secretary of State no later than ninety days prior to the election during which it will be voted on.

Laws or amendments that make it onto the ballot are then referred to as "measures." For example, in the 2014 elections, an initiative proposing a law that elementary and secondary school classes had to begin after Labor Day was referred to as Measure 8.[5]

Once the Secretary of State has received the required number of signatures, the Legislative Council[6] creates a fiscal impact statement to accompany the measure. If a measure is approved by voters, it goes into effect thirty days after the election during which it was approved.

III. Researching North Dakota Ballot Measures

A. Approved Ballot Measures

As you delve into ballot measures, keep in mind that research surrounding approved North Dakota ballot measures is a straightforward process. The

---

5. This measure did not pass. Further, note that items placed on the ballot by the legislature, rather than through the citizen petition process, are also called "measures." So, for example, a 2014 legislatively referred amendment regarding abortion that made national headlines was referred to as Measure 1.

6. The Legislative Council is discussed in further detail in Chapter 6, North Dakota Statutes.

process does not require any additional strategy outside of that discussed in previous chapters, unless you are conducting research for historical purposes. This is because once a measure has been approved, either it becomes a statutory law or constitutional amendment like any other in the state or it repeals a law, in which case you no longer need to be concerned with it. In other words, the fact that a law or amendment began as a ballot measure has no impact on its enforceability. Therefore, researching the state constitution, as discussed in Chapter 5, or state statutes, as discussed in Chapter 6, will cover your bases so long as you ensure that you update your research, as discussed in Chapter 12, to avoid missing any very recently passed ballot measures.

B. Upcoming Ballot Measures

Given that approved ballot measures become part of constitutional or statutory research, researching North Dakota ballot measures themselves is more about keeping up with potential changes in the law that may currently be in the works. Because there are no limits in North Dakota on the subject matter of initiatives and referendums, an upcoming ballot measure could potentially address any topic. On the other hand, because very few measures actually make it onto the ballot in a given year, ensuring that you have found all of them is not an onerous process. For example, during the 2014 election year,[7] only nine measures appeared on the ballot, including both legislatively referred measures and citizen-initiated measures; this was the highest number of measures since 1996.

Far and away, the best source for researching upcoming North Dakota ballot measures is the "Ballot Measures" section of the website for the North Dakota Secretary of State.[8] When applicable,[9] measures that have been approved for an upcoming ballot appear on the front page of this section of the website. The information provided includes the text of the law (if a legislatively referred measure) or the text of the petition (if an initiative or a referendum), analyses

---

7. Typically, North Dakota holds two elections every two years, a primary election in the late spring and a general election in the fall of even years. Ballot measures may be present during both elections. For example, in the 2014 election year, one measure appeared on the ballot during the primary election, and eight appeared on the ballot during the general election. If a special election is held outside of these ordinary times, measures may be present on that ballot as well.

8. *See* https://vip.sos.nd.gov/PortalListDetails.aspx?ptlhPKID=117&ptlPKID=1.

9. In some years, there may be no measures on the ballot. Even when measures are approved, this approval occurs on a rolling basis, so not every measure that will eventually appear will be approved at the same time.

Figure 13-1. North Dakota Ballot of November 2014

**OFFICIAL BALLOT LANGUAGE
FOR MEASURES APPEARING ON THE
ELECTION BALLOT
November 4, 2014**

Vote by darkening the oval next to the word "YES" or "NO" following the explanation of each measure.

**Constitutional Measure No. 1
(Senate Concurrent Resolution No. 4009, 2013 Session Laws, Ch. 519)**

This constitutional measure would create and enact a new section to Article I of the North Dakota Constitution stating, "The inalienable right to life of every human being at any stage of development must be recognized and protected."

○   **YES** – means you approve the measure stated above.

○   **NO** – means you reject the measure stated above.

**Constitutional Measure No. 2
(House Concurrent Resolution No. 3006, 2013 Session Laws, Ch. 520)**

This constitutional measure would create and enact a new section to Article X of the North Dakota Constitution stating, "The state and any county, township, city, or any other political subdivision of the state may not impose any mortgage taxes or any sales or transfer taxes on the mortgage or transfer of real property."

○   **YES** – means you approve the measure stated above.

○   **NO** – means you reject the measure stated above.

Source: https://vip.sos.nd.gov/pdfs/measures%20Info/2014%20General/Official_Ballot_Language_2014_General.pdf.

explaining the impact of the measures, the full text of the measures, and the official ballot text. The text that will appear on the ballot is, essentially, a much abbreviated version of the full text and analysis, summarizing at the most basic level what the voters are voting on.

Figure 13-1 contains part of the official ballot for the November 2014 North Dakota elections, demonstrating two proposed constitutional measures.

Even when no measures have yet been approved for an upcoming ballot, the North Dakota Secretary of State website includes a wealth of information on both the initiative and referendum process as well as ballot measures that are in the works. For example, under the "Ballot Petitions Being Reviewed" link, you can find signed petitions that have been submitted to the Secretary of State for review as well as a timeline for when the review process will be completed (recall that a measure is not officially on the ballot until the signatures have been submitted to and approved by the Secretary of State). Under "Ballot Petitions Being Circulated," you can find petitions for which signatures are currently being collected. The "How to Place a Measure on a Ballot" link provides information about the process for initiating or referring law, as well as helpful materials like a "Petition Drafting Tool" and sample petitions.

In researching the potential impact of a given ballot measure, the information provided on the Secretary of State's website is a good start. To more thoroughly understand the possible impact of a given ballot measure, you will likely want to engage with outside analyses as well. The National Conference of State Legislatures[10] publishes analyses of some ballot measures on its website as does the Initiative and Referendum Institute.[11] Note that both of these websites have nationwide coverage and are not comprehensive as to every measure that may be proposed in a given year.

A particularly valuable resource for learning more about ballot measures is Ballotpedia.org, a website similar to Wikipedia.org that is devoted to local, state, and federal politics and elections. Like Wikipedia.org, Ballotpedia.org allows individual users to edit pages and should not be treated as an authoritative source; however, the site is arguably a bit more trustworthy than Wikipedia.org because submissions are fact checked by the site's professional editing staff. Therefore, while caution is warranted, the site remains an excellent source for gaining background information on a variety of political topics, including ballot measures.

On the front page of the Ballotpedia.org website, you can click on "State," which will provide you with a dropdown menu. One of the choices in the menu is "Ballot Measures." That page provides a variety of information, including recent news, upcoming election dates, a hyperlinked list of ballot measures organized by type, a chart for topics that are currently considered "hot" nationwide, and, at the bottom of the page, a hyperlinked list of all of the states that allow initiatives and referendums.

The Ballotpedia.org website is also searchable, and searching for a particular ballot measure can provide a large amount of information such as a summary of the measure in question, arguments for and against the measure, and election results if the measure has already appeared on the ballot. For example, Figure 13-2 shows the table of contents for the Ballotpedia.org webpage devoted to Measure 1, a ballot measure that appeared on the November 2014 North Dakota ballot.[12]

To research upcoming ballot measures, you may also want to research periodicals, including newspaper and magazine stories. Lexis includes a "Legal News" category, which can be found by clicking "Browse," then "Sources," then

---

10. *See* http://www.ncsl.org.

11. *See* http://www.iandrinstitute.org.

12. This measure was defeated with 161,303 voting against and 90,224 voting in favor.

Figure 13-2. Ballotpedia Table of Contents

Contents [hide]

1 Election results

2 Text of the measure

    2.1 Ballot title

    2.2 Constitutional changes

3 Background

    3.1 "Personhood" measures

    3.2 Measure 1 of 1972

    3.3 2013 bills

4 Support

    4.1 Supporters

        4.1.1 Officials

        4.1.2 Organizations

            4.1.2.1 Churches

    4.2 Arguments

    4.3 Campaign contributions

5 Opposition

    5.1 Opponents

    5.2 Arguments

    5.3 Campaign contributions

6 Media editorial positions

    6.1 Opposition

7 Polls

8 Path to the ballot

    8.1 Senate vote

    8.2 House vote

9 See also

10 External links

    10.1 Basic information

    10.2 Support

    10.3 Opposition

11 References

Source: http://ballotpedia.org/North_Dakota_%22Life_Begins_at_Conception%22_Amendment,_Measure_1_(2014).

"By Category." Westlaw has a "Legal Newspapers and Newsletters" database found by browsing in "Secondary Sources." You may also want to simply use Google to find articles in the larger local newspapers like the Bismarck Tribune, the Forum of Fargo-Moorhead, and the Grand Forks Herald.

C. Past Ballot Measures

For most ordinary legal research, you will not likely need past ballot measures. However, they can be useful in compiling a legislative history or in understanding the political history of the state, which may help you predict future developments. For example, if you were analyzing the likelihood that a new ballot measure would pass, it might be helpful to know that a similar measure was defeated in the past. The remainder of this chapter explains four sources of information on past ballot measures: (1) the North Dakota Secretary of State website; (2) the National Conference of State Legislatures; (3) the Initiative & Referendum Institute; and (4) *Laws of North Dakota.*

First, the "Election Results" page of the North Dakota Secretary of State website[13] provides election results and materials, including ballot measures, back to 2000. For example, to find the text of measures that appeared on the November 2008 ballot, first click on the link for "Election Results" and then "2000-2008 Election Results." From there, click on the link for the 2008 November election, which brings you to a page describing such information as who was up for election that year and how many people voted. Included on this page, under the "Resources" heading is a link called "Statewide Measure Information," which will take you to the text of the ballot measures as well as the election result for each measure. Figure 13-3 shows part of the page that includes the measure text and election results for the 2008 elections.

Second, the National Conference of State Legislatures maintains a "Ballot Measures Database" on its website that includes ballot measures for all states going back more than a century. The database is searchable by date, topic, year, election type (e.g., primary, general, or special), and measure type (e.g., initiative, legislative referendum, or popular referendum). Results include a summary of the measure, whether it passed, and the percentage of those who voted in favor of the measures.

Finding the database by browsing from the National Conference of State Legislature's home page[14] is not intuitive; instead, your best bet is to type "ballot

---

13. *See* https://vip.sos.nd.gov/PortalListDetails.aspx?ptlhPKID=62&ptlPKID=4.
14. *See* http://www.ncsl.org.

Figure 13-3. North Dakota 2008 Measure Information Page

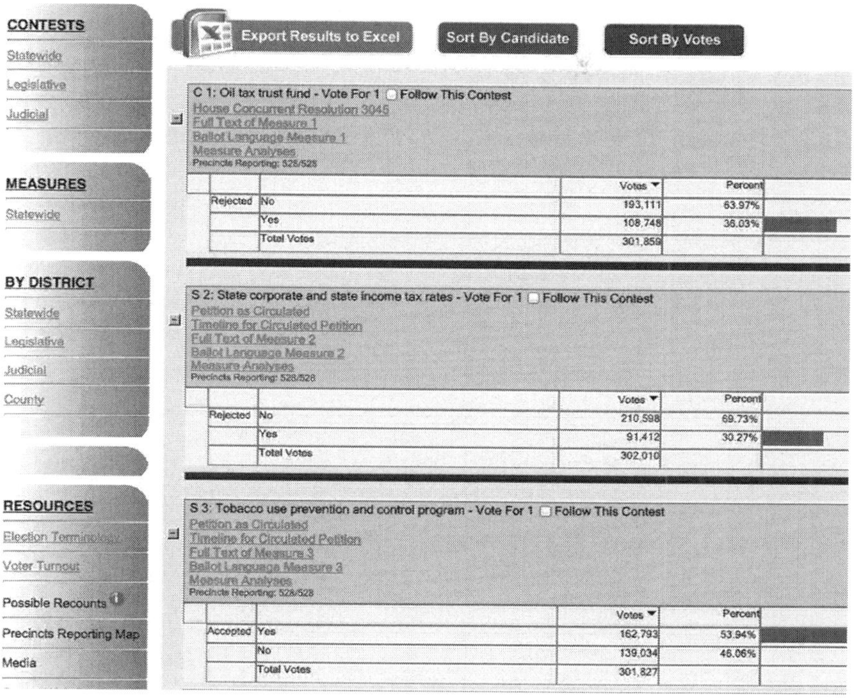

CONTESTS
Statewide
Legislative
Judicial

MEASURES
Statewide

BY DISTRICT
Statewide
Legislative
Judicial
County

RESOURCES
Election Terminology
Voter Turnout
Possible Recounts
Precincts Reporting Map
Media

Export Results to Excel | Sort By Candidate | Sort By Votes

C 1: Oil tax trust fund - Vote For 1 ☐ Follow This Contest
House Concurrent Resolution 3045
Full Text of Measure 1
Ballot Language Measure 1
Measure Analyses
Precincts Reporting: 528/528

		Votes ▼	Percent
Rejected	No	193,111	63.97%
	Yes	108,748	36.03%
	Total Votes	301,859	

S 2: State corporate and state income tax rates - Vote For 1 ☐ Follow This Contest
Petition as Circulated
Timeline for Circulated Petition
Full Text of Measure 2
Ballot Language Measure 2
Measure Analyses
Precincts Reporting: 528/528

		Votes ▼	Percent
Rejected	No	210,598	69.73%
	Yes	91,412	30.27%
	Total Votes	302,010	

S 3: Tobacco use prevention and control program - Vote For 1 ☐ Follow This Contest
Petition as Circulated
Timeline for Circulated Petition
Full Text of Measure 3
Ballot Language Measure 3
Measure Analyses
Precincts Reporting: 528/528

		Votes ▼	Percent
Accepted	Yes	162,793	53.94%
	No	139,034	46.06%
	Total Votes	301,827	

Source: http://results.sos.nd.gov/resultsSW.aspx?text=BQ&type=SW&map=CTY&eid=1.

measures" in the search box on the home page. This will take you to a list of results, the first of which should be the "Ballot Measures Database." However, if you prefer to find the database by browsing (for example, if you want to see other potentially helpful materials offered on this website), first click on "Research," then, in the Navigation side bar, "Elections and Campaigns." From there, click on "Initiative and Referendum," and scroll down to the heading "Databases." In addition to the "Ballot Measures Database," you will also find databases on legislation impacting the initiative and referendum process (for example, laws changing the petition signature requirements).

Third, the Initiative & Referendum Institute also contains a list of ballot measures for each state, although it includes only citizen-initiated initiatives and referendums (i.e., legislatively referred measures are not included). This site is not as up-to-date as the National Conference of State Legislature's database, but it has the benefit of listing all past initiatives and referendums together in one place. To access the list for North Dakota from the Initiative & Referendum Institute home page,[15] click on "State I&R," then click on "North Dakota" on the map provided. A link listing initiatives from 1918-1998 is provided on the left.

Finally, the full text of ballot measures, both approved and disapproved, are included in the *Laws of North Dakota*, the official publication for North Dakota's session laws.[16] This publication is available back to the 1985-86 legislative session on the North Dakota Legislative Branch website.[17] If you know in which year your ballot measure appeared, use the link for "Session Laws" at the bottom of the page to navigate to the appropriate legislative session.[18] After you have navigated to the appropriate legislative session, click on the link for "Chapter Categories." Near the end of the list, you will find categories for "Initiated Measures Approved," "Initiated Measures Disapproved," "Referred Measures Approved," and "Referred Measures Disapproved."

If you do not already know the year for your measure, instead click on the "Research Center" link and then scroll down to "Measures Before the Voters." This link will take you to a chronological list of measures that have been placed before the voters since 1889, including both legislatively referred measures and citizen-initiated initiatives and referendums. The list provides a brief description of each measure, the method of proposal (for example by legislative referral or initiative), the vote tally for and against, and whether the amendment was accepted or rejected (designated by an "A" or an "R").

This list of measures only includes a brief description of measures so to access the full text, you will need to consult the *Laws of North Dakota*. As stated previously, this document is available back to 1985 on the North Dakota Legislative Branch website. For older copies, consult the print version or, if your library has a subscription, HeinOnline, which includes coverage back to 1889.

---

15. *See* http://www.iandrinstitute.org.
16. For more on session laws, see Chapter 6: Statutes.
17. *See* http://www.legis.nd.gov.
18. Note that most measures appear in even years because they are typically put on the ballot during the primary or regular election. Session laws, however, are published in odd years; look for the year that directly follows the election year for your ballot measure.

Chapter 14

Oil and Gas Law

I. Introduction

This chapter covers legal research in a substantive area of law important to many North Dakota lawyers, oil and gas.

Oil and gas is a key industry in North Dakota. Currently, oil in the Bakken Formation in western North Dakota drives the state's oil industry. The name "Bakken" is from North Dakota farmer Henry O. Bakken, who owned the land where the oil was first discovered in the 1950s.[1] Though it was discovered in the 1950s, oil in the Bakken was not commercially recoverable until the late 2000s with hydraulic fracturing ("fracking"), a major advancement in drilling technology. In April 2013, the United States Geological Survey estimated that there are more than seven billion recoverable barrels of oil in the Bakken Formation.[2] This makes the Bakken the largest reserve of oil discovered in the lower forty-eight. The U.S. Energy Information Administration estimates that North Dakota is now the second-largest oil producer in the United States, second only to Texas.[3]

The Bakken-inspired oil boom has affected just about every aspect of life in the western part of the state; it has dramatically increased the need for oil and gas related legal services. As a result, some familiarity with oil and gas law research is an important part of the North Dakota lawyer's skillset. This chapter provides a basic overview of the regulatory landscape of oil and gas in North Dakota and where to find oil and gas law.

---

1. You can learn more background about the Bakken at http://bakkenshale.com/.
2. This and more information on the Bakken is available from the U.S. Geological Survey at http://www.usgs.gov/faq/categories/9778/3144 and from the Department of the Interior at http://www.doi.gov/news/pressreleases/usgs-releases-new-oil-and-gas-assessment-for-bakken-and-three-forks-formations.cfm.
3. Crude oil production statistics by state are available from the U.S. Energy Information Administration at http://www.eia.gov/dnav/pet/pet_crd_crpdn_adc_mbblpd_m.htm.

II. Regulation of Oil and Gas in North Dakota

The North Dakota Industrial Commission — through its Department of Mineral Resources, Oil and Gas Division — oversees the oil and gas industry in North Dakota.[4] In carrying out its mission, the Oil and Gas Division regulates drilling, oil and gas production, field processing and transportation of extracted oil and gas, and surface activities of oil companies. This division locates and maintains records of wells. It also issues and oversees permits to drill, recomplete,[5] and drill horizontally.

While regulation of oil and gas drilling is typically left to the states, federal government agencies are also involved in various aspects of the oil and gas industry. These agencies include the Bureau of Land Management, the Federal Energy Regulatory Commission, and the Environmental Protection Agency.

III. Getting Started on Oil and Gas Research

If you are new to oil and gas law, then your first stop should be secondary sources. Recall that secondary sources provide explanations of the law and sometimes cites to primary authority. There is one North Dakota-specific secondary source on this topic, Professor David Saxowsky's website on oil and gas law in North Dakota, which is posted through North Dakota State University.[6] Professor Saxowsky's site explains the basics of North Dakota's oil and gas industry, from exploration to production. He provides both commentary as well as citations to relevant portions of the North Dakota Century Code.

Of particular interest to North Dakota lawyers is the Rocky Mountain Mineral Law Foundation's *Development Issues in Major Shale Plays* (2014). It offers an in-depth exploration of the legal issues that have arisen as extraction of oil from shale has become a reality in the Bakken and other places like it. Included are sections on legal and regulatory developments relating to horizontal drilling and hydraulic fracturing.

Two general treatises may be useful. While not specifically targeted to North Dakota, Patrick H. Martin and Bruce M. Kramer's Williams & Meyers Oil and Gas Law (LexisNexis Matthew Bender 2013) is a comprehensive treatise of oil and gas transactions frequently cited by courts. It covers insurance, leasing,

---

4. The website is www.dmr.nd.gov/oilgas/.
5. Recomplete means to adjust a well for production from another area.
6. You can access the site at https://www.ag.ndsu.edu/NDOilandGasLaw.

and government regulation. It also includes forms and all relevant statutes from oil and gas producing states. Additionally, Owen Anderson and Eugene Kuntz's *Kuntz, A Treatise on the Law of Oil and Gas* (Anderson Pub. Co. 2010 ed.) is increasingly cited by courts. It offers a survey of oil and gas conveyancing and operations, including insurance, leasing, and government regulation. It, too, includes forms and all relevant statutes from oil and gas producing states.

For a more comprehensive list of secondary sources relating to oil and gas law, see the appendix to this chapter.

IV. Where to Find Oil and Gas Law

A. Statutes and Regulations

The state legislature and the Department of Natural Resources regulate North Dakota's oil and gas industry. As a result, both statutes and regulations impact oil and gas in North Dakota. Chapter 38 of the North Dakota Century Code, Mining and Oil and Gas Production, applies to mining and oil and gas production. As noted in Chapter 6 of this book, there are several ways to locate relevant statutes. Even without knowing which chapter pertains to oil and gas, you could locate Chapter 38 of the Century Code by looking up "oil and gas" in the Century Code index. Alternatively, you could look on the legislature's website. This approach is more economical than using a commercial provider like Lexis or Westlaw.

Title 43 of the North Dakota Administrative Code, the Industrial Commission, applies to oil and gas. As noted in Chapter 8, the chapter of this book that addresses administrative law, there are several ways to locate relevant regulations, just as there are several ways to locate relevant statutes. The most economical is to check the print regulations or to look on the legislature's website. Note that, while Chapter 38 of the Century Code has the term "oil and gas" in the title, Title 43 does not. Instead, it is titled "Industrial Commission" for the body that directly regulates oil and gas in North Dakota. Because the relevant title in the administrative code is not as immediately apparent as Chapter 38 of the Century Code, knowing that the Industrial Commission regulates oil and gas is helpful.

While regulation of oil and gas is largely left to the states, there are some applicable federal statutes and regulations. Relevant statutes are scattered in a few different places in the United States Code, but the bulk of the applicable statutes appear in Title 30, Mineral Lands and Mining. To find this title, and other relevant statutes, you can search Congress's website or refer to the United States Code index. Many of the relevant regulations are under Title

Figure 14-1. The Energy and Environment Practice Area on Westlaw

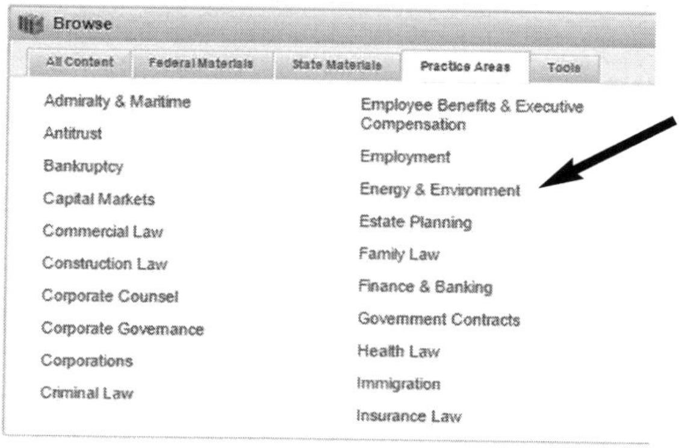

Source: Westlaw. Reprinted with permission of Thomson Reuters.

18, Federal Energy Commission, and Title 43, Public Lands: Interior. You can find relevant regulations by searching the index of the *Code of Federal Regulations*.

Finally, the Utilities Law Reporter covers the regulation of gas and electric utilities. It contains relevant categories of information for natural gas and electricity, including the full text of federal statutes and regulations.

B. Cases

Chapter 11 of this book, Researching Case Law, covered how to find cases using digests and text searches. Those tools will help you find oil and gas case law. In addition, some specialized tools are available as well. Westlaw offers a specialized database for Energy and Environment. You can access it by clicking on "Practice Area." See Figure 14-1. Similarly, you can search Lexis's Energy and Utilities practice area by browsing and clicking on "Practice Area" and then "Energy and Utilities." See Figure 14-2. Also, as noted above, the Utilities Law Reporter covers the regulation of gas and electric utilities. In addition to federal statutes and regulations, the reporter includes state and federal court decisions and Federal Energy Regulatory Commission orders and opinions.

Figure 14-2. The Energy and Utilities Practice Area on Lexis

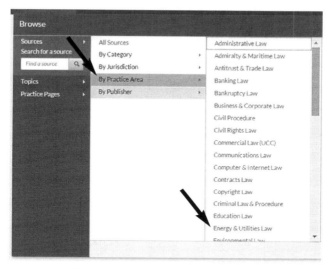

Source: Lexis Advance. Reprinted with permission from Reed Elsevier.

Appendix: Selected Secondary Sources on Oil and Gas Law

Listed below are selected secondary sources on oil and gas law. The list is not a complete list of all available sources; rather, it is a selection of some of the most highly regarded sources.

North Dakota Sources

- David Saxowsky's online primer, complete with cites to the North Dakota Century Code, is available online at https://www.ag.ndsu.edu/NDOilandGasLaw (last visited July 20, 2015). This source includes information on exploration and production, surface rights, mineral rights, the role of the Industrial Commission, and more.

Other Secondary Sources

- Owen L. Anderson & Eugene O. Kuntz, *Kuntz, A Treatise on the Law of Oil and Gas* (Anderson Pub. Co. 2010 ed.)

  This treatise is a survey of oil and gas conveyancing and operations, including insurance, leasing, and government regulation. It also includes forms and all relevant statutes from oil and gas producing states.

- Patrick H. Martin & Bruce M. Kramer, Williams & Meyers Oil and Gas Law (LexisNexis Matthew Bender 2013)

  Frequently cited by courts, this treatise of oil and gas transactions includes conveyancing, leasing, pooling and unitization, gas purchase contracts, taxation, accounting techniques, financial administration, title examination, administering estates and preparing wills and trusts. It also includes forms.

- David J. Muchow & William A. Mogel, *Energy Law and Transactions* (LexisNexis Matthew Bender 2015)

  This source covers traditional and nontraditional energy sources, from exploration and production to consumption by the end user.

- Rocky Mountain Mineral Law Foundation, *Development Issues in Major Shale Plays* (2014)

- Rocky Mountain Mineral Law Foundation, *Oil and Gas Agreements: Contracting for Goods, Services, and People* (2013)

- Rocky Mountain Mineral Law Foundation, *Due Diligence in Oil and Gas Transactions* (2011)

- Rocky Mountain Mineral Law Foundation, *Oil and Gas Agreements: Midstream and Marketing* (2011)

- Rocky Mountain Mineral Law Foundation, *Oil and Gas Agreements: The Exploration Phase* (2010)

- W.L. Summers, *The Law of Oil and Gas* (3d ed. 2004)

  This multi-volume treatise covers property interests, drilling, leases, remedies, taxation, and transportation. It also includes forms.

Chapter 15

Indian Law

I. Introduction

In recent years, more and more legal researchers have come to recognize the importance of Indian law.[1] This is especially true in states like North Dakota that have a large Native American population. In fact, three states with significant Native American populations — New Mexico, South Dakota, and Washington — have recently added questions about Indian law to their state bar examinations. Thus, although the topic of Indian law is not specific to North Dakota, this chapter reflects the importance of this type of law to the people of the state.

The phrase *Indian law* is broad and may refer to two different bodies of law. The first, more appropriately deemed *federal Indian law*, refers to the law governing the relationship between the federal government and Indian tribes. The second, *tribal law*, refers to the laws created by individual tribes to govern their members.[2] This chapter addresses both types of law.

II. Researching Federal Indian Law

Because federal Indian law is different from other types of federal law only in the sense that it is about a specific subject matter, traditional legal research techniques will serve the federal Indian law researcher well. The following sections summarize some important sources for researching federal Indian law and explain how to access them; however, you may want to refresh your memory on the research process and strategies by consulting Chapter 1, Research

---

1. Note that "Indian law," as opposed to "Native American law," is the commonly accepted parlance among scholars and practitioners in this area.
2. Currently, there are more than 560 federally-recognized tribes and Alaska Native Villages that exercise their right to sovereignty.

Process, and Chapter 2, Research Techniques. Additionally, the following chapter, Chapter 16, Federal Equivalents, will assist you in understanding the main sources in which you will find federal law.

A. Secondary Sources Related to Federal Indian Law

General secondary sources, such as those discussed in Chapter 4, Secondary Sources, can certainly be of use in researching federal Indian law. For example, the two key legal encyclopedias discussed in that chapter, *American Jurisprudence 2d* (Am. Jur. 2d) and *Corpus Juris Secundum* (C.J.S.), both have topic headings for "Indians." By developing good search terms and being sure to include "Indian" or "Native American," you can find secondary sources related to federal Indian law.

However, some secondary sources related specifically to federal Indian law are worth noting. These sources are discussed in this section. Most of these sources are available only in print; where they are available online, it is noted.

1. *Cohen's Handbook of Federal Indian Law*

Cohen's Handbook of Federal Indian Law is considered the most comprehensive and authoritative treatise available on federal Indian law. The treatise covers the relationships among tribes, the federal government, and the state and covers a large variety of topics: civil and criminal jurisdiction, water rights, economic development, environmental regulation, gaming, tribal property rights, and more. Detailed overviews of the various topics are provided as well as a wealth of references to primary sources. The treatise is updated regularly and includes a table of contents and an index as well as a table of cases and a table of statutes.

Because of its importance, most academic law libraries will own a copy of *Cohen's Handbook of Federal Indian Law* in print. It is also available online on Lexis. The easiest way to find it on Lexis is to click on "Browse," then "Source." Then type "Cohen's Handbook of Federal Indian Law" into the search box that appears. The Lexis version allows for full-text searching; it also includes the table of contents but not the index or other tables.

2. Other Treatises

The *American Indian Law Deskbook* is an up-to-date treatise published by the Conference of Western Attorneys General. It is probably second only to Cohen's in its usefulness and comprehensiveness. This treatise explains both federal statutory and case law related to the development of Indian law as well as compiling and analyzing major federal and state court cases. It includes a table of contents, an index, and a table of cases, public laws, and regulations.

American Indian Law in a Nutshell provides an overview of basic components of federal Indian law, including the relationship between the federal government and tribes, criminal and civil jurisdiction, and some specialized topics like taxation, gaming, and Alaska Native law. It includes an index and table of contents. Note that although books in the "Nutshell" series are not considered treatises, strictly speaking, this book is consistently listed as one of the key sources by expert federal Indian law researchers.

The *Rights of Indians and Tribes* is another popular, comprehensive guide covering many of the same topics as the other treatises already discussed. A key difference is the format of this source; it is written in a question-and-answer style and is specifically aimed primarily at a non-scholarly audience. This user-friendly, plain language style might make it a good first stop for those researchers with little experience in federal Indian law.

In addition to these popular sources in federal Indian law, you should be sure to check your library catalog to see what is available. Some treatises, like those discussed here, cover federal Indian law generally, but there are also subject-specific treatises on the market such as *Children, Tribes, and States: Adoption and Custody Conflicts Over American Indian Children* and *Handbook of Federal Indian Education Laws*.

3. Legal Encyclopedias and Dictionaries

As already noted, both Am. Jur. 2d and C.J.S. include topic headings for "Indians." In addition, a few legal encyclopedias and dictionaries have been published specifically covering federal Indian law.

The *Encyclopedia of United States Indian Policy and Law* is a two-volume set focused on the relationship of the federal government with tribes, particularly from a political, sociological, and historic vantage point. It includes both essays and regular A-to-Z style entries.

The *Encyclopedia of Native American Legal Tradition* provides an overview of over twenty major Native American tribes, including their political and legal traditions. It also describes major cases, statutes, and treaties, and profiles some of the major individual figures in the development of Indian law and policy.

Finally, *Native Americans and the Law: A Dictionary*, acts as both a dictionary and an encyclopedia. It not only defines key terms, but also includes more encyclopedic entries describing important information such as major court decisions, tribes, and government agencies.

4. Legal Periodicals

a. Law Reviews and Journals

Because most law reviews and journals cover a wide range of legal topics, federal Indian law topics could be located in any number of different publications. A comprehensive search of law reviews and journals should therefore apply the techniques discussed in Chapter 4, Secondary Sources.

Nonetheless, a couple of journals specialize in federal Indian law and may be worth browsing or searching individually. The *American Indian Law Review* is edited and published by students at the University of Oklahoma College of Law and is available online on Lexis and Westlaw. The *American Indian Law Journal* is an online journal published by students, faculty, and practitioners through the Seattle University School of Law.[3]

b. Other Legal Periodicals

There are several good resources for news and updates related to federal Indian law. These resources are excellent for keeping abreast of current and ongoing legal issues.

The National Indian Law Library (N.I.L.L.) publishes the *Indian Law Bulletins*, a collection of newsletters that provide information about new developments in Indian law. Newsletters are available on the following topics: U.S. Supreme Court; Federal Courts of Appeal; Federal Trial Courts; State Courts; U.S. Regulatory Information; U.S. Legislation; News Bulletin; and Law Review/Bar Journal Articles. The content and publication schedule differs for each bulletin, but that information as well as both current issues and archives for each bulletin can be found on the N.I.L.L. website.[4]

Mealey's Native American Law Report is a monthly newsletter reporting on litigation in federal, state, and tribal courts. It includes articles and case summaries on a wide variety of issues and also reprints some court and agency opinions. It is published by LexisNexis; it is available in print or may be purchased as an e-book with updates sent via email.

Another monthly newsletter is the *Native American Law Digest*, which provides summaries of recent legal developments and cases, both state and federal, related to Indian law. It is available only in print.

---

3. The website for the journal is http://www.law.seattleu.edu/academics/enrichment/journals/ailj.
4. The address is http://www.narf.org/nill/bulletins/.

In addition, more general news-oriented publications available may also cover legal issues. For example, Indian Country Today is an online site that publishes a free weekly e-newsletter covering a wide range of both news and entertainment topics. Similarly, Indian Country Communications, Inc. publishes the newspaper *News From Indian Country*, in both a print version and a digital version, fourteen times a year.[5]

B. Primary Sources Related to Federal Indian Law

As with all other areas of federal law, federal Indian law can be found chiefly in statutes, cases, and administrative regulations. In addition, *treaties* — agreements between sovereign states — are important in federal Indian law research as they set the groundwork for the relationship between the federal government and various Native American tribes.

The techniques explained and discussed elsewhere in this book apply to researching federal Indian law as well. It is helpful to know, too, that the major online services have organized their materials in such a way as to make access to federal Indian law materials more direct than simply going through the general federal statute, case, administrative regulation, and treaty databases. This section discusses the collections those services offer and how to access them. Note that all of the services discussed here have collections of primary and secondary material for both federal Indian law and tribal law. Only those collections related to primary federal Indian law are discussed in this section; secondary sources were discussed in the previous section, and tribal law resources will be discussed in Part III of this chapter. Additionally, although most of the resources discussed here are also available in print, electronic methods provide far more widespread and easier access, so print resources are not discussed.

1. Federal Indian Law Materials on Lexis

To access federal Indian law materials on Lexis, from the home page, first click on "Browse," then "Practice Pages." Next, click on "By Practice Area," and, finally, "Native American." These steps will take you to a page showing Lexis's collections of primary and secondary materials for both federal Indian law and tribal law. Figure 15-1 shows a screenshot of Lexis's resources in this area.

The database "Native American Cases, Federal and State," will allow you to search for Indian law cases without having to go through one of the larger,

---

5. The website for the digital edition is http://digital.newsfromindiancountry.com/app.asp?RelId=5.5.7p1.5.

Figure 15-1. Lexis's Federal Indian Law and Tribal Law Collections

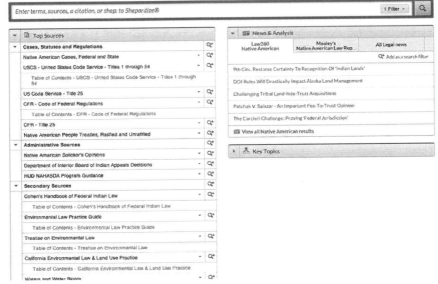

Source: Lexis Advance. Reprinted with permission from Reed Elsevier.

more general case databases, thus likely improving the accuracy of your searches. In addition to listing the general databases for United States statutes (United States Code Service) and administrative regulations (Code of Federal Regulations), Lexis also provides separate links to Title 25 for each of these bodies of law; Title 25 is the main title governing Indian Law matters.[6]

Under the heading "Administrative Sources," Lexis also includes a few important databases. As one example, the "Native American Solicitor's Opinions" database includes opinions from 1917 to 1974 issued by the Solicitor of the Department of the Interior.

Lexis also has the administrative decisions from the Interior Board of Indian Appeals. Chapter 8, Administrative Law, explained that state administrative agencies are often empowered with the quasi-judicial authority to decide disputes between members of the public and their agency. Many federal agencies also have that power. The main federal actors in charge of handling federal Indian law are the Bureau of Indian Affairs (B.I.A.) and the Assistant Secretary of Indian Affairs, both of which are housed in the U.S. Department of the Interior. The

---

6. Note, however, that Indian law matters may be discussed in other titles as well, so also conduct a search in the full databases if you do not find what you are looking for under Title 25.

Interior Board of Indian Appeals hears appeals from both B.I.A. decisions and decisions of the Assistant Secretary of Indian Affairs. It also hears appeals on some Indian-related decisions handed down by Administrative Law Judges in other agencies. Lexis's database of decisions goes back to midway through 1969.

Additionally, the database "HUD NAHASDA Program Guidance" includes guidance documents and opinions back to late 1997 from the Office of Native American Programs, which is housed under the U.S. Department of Housing and Urban Development (HUD). NAHASDA refers to the Native American Housing Assistance and Self Determination Act of 1996, which created block grant programs for providing housing assistance to Native Americans.

Finally, the database "Native American People Treaties, Ratified and Unratified," contains the full text of historic treaties drawn up from 1787 to 1883.

2. Federal Indian Law Materials on Westlaw

To access federal Indian law materials on Westlaw, from the home page, first click on the tab for "Practice Areas." This will take you to a hyperlinked list of topics; choose "Native American Law." Westlaw's collections of primary and secondary materials for both federal Indian law and tribal law are collected on this page. Figure 15-2 provides a screenshot of Westlaw's "Native American Law" page.

Databases exist for "Federal Native American Law Cases," "Federal Native American Law Statutes & Court Rules," and "Federal Native American Law Regulations." While you can also access federal Indian law cases through the large, general federal databases of cases, statutes, and regulations, using these more specialized databases will help to narrow your results and will not require you to remember to put "Indian" or "Native American" into each search query. Additionally, like Lexis, Westlaw also has the administrative decisions from the Interior Board of Indian Appeals; Westlaw's database goes back to 1970.

Finally, Westlaw also has a database called "Native American Law Treaties." As can be seen in Figure 15-2, this database is listed off to the right side of the Native American Law page, rather than with the other databases. Westlaw's collection includes all Native American treaties with the U.S. government back to 1797.

3. Federal Indian Law Materials on HeinOnline

HeinOnline also has an extensive collection of current and historical federal Indian law and tribal law materials in its "American Indian Law Collection."[7]

---

7. A full description of HeinOnline's collection is available online at http://www.heinonline.org/HeinDocs/AmericanIndianLawCollection.pdf.

Figure 15-2. Westlaw's Federal Indian Law and Tribal Law Collections

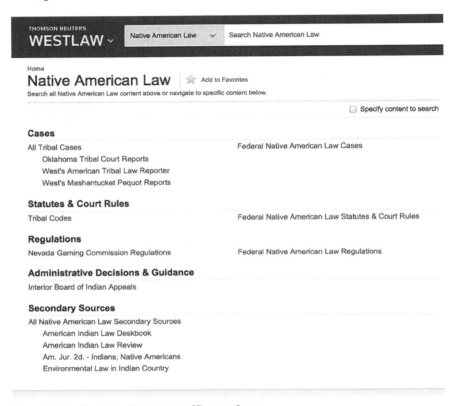

Source: Westlaw. Reprinted with permission of Thomson Reuters

HeinOnline's collection includes such materials as statutes and administrative regulations, compiled legislative histories, historical laws and papers, some federal case law, treaties, and decisions of certain administrative agencies such as the Interior Board of Indian Appeals, the Interior Board of Land Appeals, and the Indian Claims Commission.[8] While Lexis and Westlaw will likely be easier to use in searching for those current materials in which coverage overlaps, HeinOnline's collection is an unparalleled online resource for researchers in need of historical materials.

---

8. The Indian Claims Commission was disbanded in 1978, but from 1946 to 1978, it was the chief means by which claims against the United States by Indian tribes were heard and adjudicated.

4. Free Online Resources

Like state law, much federal law is available for free online. Although free online services tend to have somewhat less searching capability than the commercial services, many free services are well designed and comprehensive. In fact, a few types of primary sources that are not fully available in the commercial services are available for free online.

One of the best free resources for those researching federal law, including federal Indian law, is FDsys, a website created by the U.S. Government Publishing Office.[9] This site publishes statutes and administrative regulations. Statutes and administrative regulations are also available on Cornell University's Legal Information Institute website.[10] The Center for Regulatory Effectiveness lists the popular names of laws related to Native Americans and provides links to free online versions of the laws.[11] The U.S. Department of the Interior publishes online its Solicitor's opinions back to 1993.[12] Oklahoma State University Library has digitized and made available online[13] one of the most comprehensive resources for Native American treaties, *Indian Affairs: Laws and Treaties*.[14]

III. Researching Tribal Law

Researching tribal law can be quite complex. Each tribe is a separate sovereign nation with its own law-making structure and judicial system. Moreover, compared to federal and state law, there is a dearth of primary and secondary resources as well as a large variance in what is available for each tribe. Nonetheless, the research situation has improved somewhat in recent years, particularly with the advent of electronic research. This part of the chapter discusses some of the key secondary and primary sources available; this discussion is not meant to be an exhaustive overview and not every source is covered, but it will help you to get started in your research and to become aware of the type of materials that are available.

---

9. *See* http://www.gpo.gov/fdsys/. Note that FDsys is slated to be replaced by a new website, www.govinfo.gov, in 2017.
10. *See* https://www.law.cornell.edu.
11. *See* http://www.thecre.com/fedlaw/legal22x.htm.
12. *See* http://www.doi.gov/solicitor/opinions.html.
13. *See* http://digital.library.okstate.edu/Kappler/.
14. Note that this publication is often referred to as "Kappler's," after its author, Charles J. Kappler.

A. Secondary Sources Related to Tribal Law

There are fewer secondary sources geared specifically toward tribal law than there are for other types of law. However, many of the sources discussed in the previous section on federal Indian law contain some tribal law information as well. For example, the *Encyclopedia of Native American Legal Traditions* and *Native Americans and the Law: A Dictionary* both provide profiles of multiple tribes, including, in some instances, the legal systems of those tribes. Similarly, the two law journals discussed, *American Indian Law Review* and *American Indian Law Journal*, while mostly focused on federal Indian law, also publish some articles on tribal law. Therefore, when researching tribal law, you should also take a look at the part of this chapter on federal Indian law in order to obtain a broader array of research resources from which to choose.

A few resources are more specifically aimed at tribal law. This section discusses some of the best options available for the tribal law researcher.

1. Important Websites

Some of the best information about tribal law can be found on the Internet. The National Indian Law Library (NILL)[15] holds a tremendous collection of both secondary and primary sources related to tribal law and has made many of the resources available online. NILL provides information on individual tribes, research guides, links to other sites, and the *Indian Law Bulletins* discussed in the previous section. NILL also has a searchable catalog including items in the collection that are not available online; some of these items may be borrowed via inter-library loan through your home library. Check with your library for details.

Another excellent online resource is the Tribal Law and Policy Institute website.[16] Here, you can find extensive information organized by jurisdiction and topic. For example, clicking on "Domestic Violence" under the link for "Topics," leads to a page summarizing major domestic violence laws and providing links to policy papers and tribal codes that address domestic violence in Indian country.

The Native American Rights Fund (NARF), the umbrella organization for NILL, also has some excellent information on its website[17] on a variety of topics related to tribal law. Of particular interest are NARF publications, which can

---

15. *See* http://www.narf.org/nill/.
16. *See* http://www.tribal-institute.org/lists/tlpi.htm.
17. *See* http://www.narf.org/our-work/publications/.

be previewed and ordered at the site; some have been made available as free downloads as well. Publications exist on such topics as the Indian Child Welfare Act, writing and revising tribal constitutions, education and more.

The federal government also provides information for and about Indian tribes on USA.gov.[18] This site lists the federally recognized tribes and provides both legal and cultural information for Native Americans.

Finally, the Native American Constitutional Law Digitization Project,[19] a joint project of the University of Oklahoma Law Center and NILL, collects and publishes both primary and secondary resources for tribal law. As will be discussed in Part III.B., the site has links for primary sources like constitutions and codes; however, it also provides research guides and links to other secondary sources.

2. Treatises, Textbooks, and Legal Periodicals

American Indian Tribal Governments is the main treatise that is consistently recommended in tribal law research guides. This publication provides an introduction to and overview of tribal governments, including both structural and legal issues. Note that this treatise does not provide a comprehensive discussion of all tribes. Instead, it examines five tribes in great depth and uses those discussions to comment on broader concepts of tribal governance.

The Tribal Legal Studies Program, a collaboration between several organizations and tribes aimed at developing legal study resources for students at tribal colleges, has also published a series of useful textbooks, with more in the works. *Introduction to Tribal Legal Studies* is probably the most useful for the general researcher, as it provides a solid introduction to and overview of tribal justice systems. Other books in the series so far include *Tribal Criminal Law and Procedure, Sharing Our Stories of Survival: Native Women Surviving Violence,* and *Structuring Sovereignty: Constitutions of Native Nations.*

The University of New Mexico School of Law publishes the Tribal Law Journal. The Tribal Law Journal is an online-only journal devoted to tribal law topics, and all issues are available for free on the journal's website.[20]

B. Primary Sources of Tribal Law

Like the federal government and the states, Native American tribes produce multiple types of primary law. The most common and important types of

---

18. *See* https://www.usa.gov/tribes.
19. *See* http://thorpe.ou.edu.
20. *See* http://lawschool.unm.edu/tlj/.

tribal law are constitutions, codes, and tribal court opinions. Some Native American tribes also have administrative agencies that produce administrative law. In addition, tribes often enter into "intergovernmental agreements"— agreements with the states or other political identities addressing areas of over-lapping concern such as education and taxation.

The accessibility of tribal law depends on the tribe in question; for certain larger tribes, access is relatively easy, while for some smaller tribes, you may need to contact the tribe itself to gain access even to common sources of law like codes. Regardless, every tribal law researcher should become very familiar with the National Indian Law Library (NILL).[21] NILL has the largest collection of tribal law in the country, and much of the collection is has been made available online or is in the process of being made available. Perhaps more importantly, NILL's librarians also provide free research assistance to attorneys and members of the public. If you cannot find legal information for the tribe you are researching, NILL's librarians should be one of your first points of contact in figuring out where to go next.

1. Constitutions and Codes

Most, though not all, Native American tribes have constitutions and codes that perform similar functions within the tribes as constitutions and codes perform in the federal and state governments. That is, the constitution acts as the overarching governing document, outlining the power of governing bodies and allocating certain rights. The codes are collections of the laws enacted by the legislative body of the tribe.[22]

In recent years, the tribes have been working with NILL and the University of Oklahoma Law Center on the Native American Constitution and Law Digitization Project (NACLDP)[23]—a project aimed at digitizing tribal constitutions and codes and making them available online. To access the available constitutions from the NACLDP home page, simply click on the link for "Constitutions" at the bottom of the page. This will take you to a page listing constitutions that have been posted by the NACLDP and links to constitutions on other sites, including both NILL and some tribal websites. Clicking on the link for

---

21. *See* http://www.narf.org/nill/.

22. Many tribes have a separation of powers similar to the federal and state governments, with an executive, legislative, and judicial branch. However, not all tribes separate these functions.

23. *See* http://thorpe.ou.edu.

Figure 15-3. NILL's Tribal Law Gateway

TRIBAL LAW GATEWAY

SEARCH TRIBAL CODES AND
CONSTITUTIONS AVAILABLE
IN OUR COLLECTION

Find Tribal Law Materials by Tribe

If your tribe is not yet linked below, please refer to our old tribal law index.

Basic Search Help
Operators and More Search Help

A B C D E F G H I–K L M N O P Q R S T U V W–Z

HOW TO FIND TRIBAL...

* Absentee-Shawnee Tribe of Indians of Oklahoma
* Affiliated Ute Citizens of the State of Utah (not recognized)
* Agdaagux Tribe of King Cove
* Agua Caliente Band of Cahuilla Indians of the Agua Caliente Indian Reservation, California
* Ak Chin Indian Community of the Maricopa (Ak Chin) Indian Reservation, Arizona
* Akiachak Native Community
* Akiak Native Community
* Alabama-Coushatta Tribe of Texas
* Alabama-Quassarte Tribal Town
* Alatna Tribal Office
* Algaaciq Tribal Government
* Allakaket Village
* Alturas Indian Rancheria, California
* Angoon Community Association
* Anvik Village
* Apache Tribe of Oklahoma
* Arapaho Tribe of the Wind River Reservation WY
* Aroostook Band of Micmacs
* Asa'Carsarmiut Tribe
* Assiniboine and Sioux Tribes of the Fort Peck Reservation, Montana
* Atqasuk Village (Atkasook)
* Augustine Band of Cahuilla Indians, California
* Bad River Band of Lake Superior Tribe of Chippewa Indians of the Bad River Reservation, Wisconsin
* Battle Mountain Band Council (see Te-Moak Tribe of Western Shoshone)

Laws: Codes & Ordinances
Constitutions
Court Opinions
Court Rules
Compacts & Agreements
Treaties
Legal Histories

Article: Researching American Indian
Tribal Law by David Selden, National
Indian Law Library. (2014)

SELECTED ONLINE
RESOURCES

Tribal Law Links / Tribal Court
Clearinghouse.

Tribal Government Links / USA.gov

Cumulative subject index for tribal
court opinions in the *Indian Law
Reporter*

If your tribe would like to participate in this online resource, please visit our Access to Tribal Law Project.

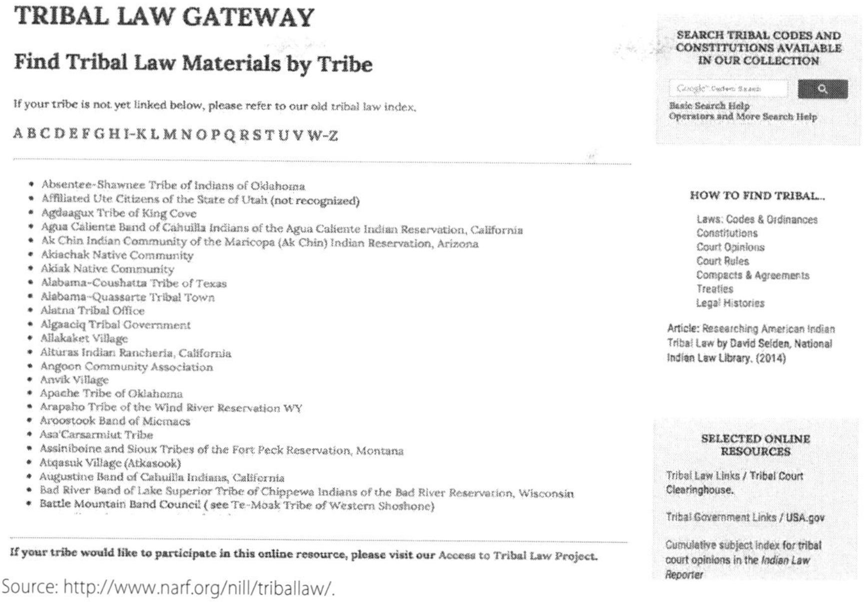

Source: http://www.narf.org/nill/triballaw/.

"Codes" from the NACLDP home page will take you to a similar page listing available tribal codes.

Consider, too, searching for constitutions and codes on the NILL site itself, as the library has many tribal constitutions and codes in print that have not yet been made available online. NILL's Tribal Law Gateway page[24] allows you to browse for materials by the name of the tribe. That page also includes a search box, which will allow you to search all of the constitutions and codes in NILL's collection. This function searches the full text of those constitutions and codes that have been made available online as well as the tables of contents for constitutions and codes in NILL's print collection. The Tribal Law Gateway page also has other valuable material such as links to research guides explaining how to search for various types of law as well as links to other important online resources and information for those charged with drafting new tribal law. Figure 15-3 shows a screenshot of part of the Tribal Law Gateway page.

For more advanced searching capabilities, use the NILL library catalog. The catalog can be accessed via a link from the NILL home page. NILL has published short video tutorials to assist researchers in using its catalog. When you click

---

24. *See* http://www.narf.org/nill/triballaw/index.html.

on the link for the catalog, a basic search box as well as links to these tutorials will be provided.

Additionally, Lexis and Westlaw have some tribal constitutions and codes. Lexis's collection is smaller; it has constitutions and/or codes for seven tribes. Coverage varies for each tribe so be sure to check the source description. Westlaw has constitutions and/or codes for twenty-four tribes. These can be found by clicking on "Tribal Codes" from Westlaw's Native American Law topic page and then selecting a tribe. (Turn back to Figure 15-2 to see that database on the Native American Law topic page.)

Throughout your research, keep in mind that you may need to contact the tribe whose law you are researching. If you cannot find a constitution or code in any of the above sources or on the tribe's home page, then you may need to request the materials. Additionally, unless a tribe publishes its own materials and states that they are official and up-to-date, you should always contact the tribe to ensure that you have the most up-to-date materials before relying on any of the materials that you find online.

2. Tribal Court Opinions

Tribal court opinions are a bit tougher to find than tribal constitutions and codes, and research is extraordinarily difficult when compared with federal and state case research. While some excellent resources certainly exist, researchers will be severely disappointed if they bring expectations developed from past experience researching federal and state cases to tribal law case research. Many tribes do not publish opinions, and there are few finding tools for those that do. Also note that many smaller tribes do not have courts at all. Nonetheless, some good research options are available for those researching certain tribes.

A great place to start if you are unsure whether the tribe you are researching publishes opinions is the NILL Tribal Law Gateway page. As discussed in the previous section and seen in Figure 15-3, the Tribal Law Gateway page contains an alphabetical listing of tribes. When you click on a tribe's name, you are provided with information on how and where to access a variety of legal information, including tribal court opinions if available.

You should also try checking with individual tribal courts. The National American Indian Court Judges Association publishes the National Directory of Tribal Justice Systems online.[25] This directory provides contact information

---

25. *See* http://www.naicja.org/directory.

for those tribes that have tribal courts. The U.S. Department of Justice provides similar information through its National Survey of Tribal Court Systems.[26]

a. Tribal Court Opinions Online

The Tribal Law and Policy Institute has a free searchable database of over 2700 tribal opinions from almost two dozen tribal courts. The database can be accessed from the Institute's home page[27] by clicking on "Tribal Law" and then selecting "Tribal Court Decisions" from the dropdown menu. Versuslaw.com has a nearly identical collection but with greater search capabilities. Versuslaw.com is a fee-based service for most users; however, the prices are lower than other fee-based services, and law students may request a password to use the service for free.

Lexis and Westlaw also collect some tribal court opinions. Lexis focuses mostly on some Montana tribes and the Eastern Band of Cherokee. Westlaw has somewhat broader coverage, providing decisions from just under two dozen tribes.

b. Tribal Court Opinions in Print

The *Indian Law Reporter* is an annual publication that collects approximately twenty-five tribal court opinions per year from a variety of tribes. NILL has created an online cumulative subject index[28] to accompany this publication. The *Indian Law Reporter* has been published since 1974, but tribal opinions were not included until volume 10.

West's Tribal Law Reporter, which is also available on Westlaw as part of its online collection, collects some tribal appellate opinions. *West's Tribal Law Reporter* has been published since 1997, but some tribal appellate courts were not included until later years.

3. Tribal Administrative Law

Although some tribes have administrative agencies and courts similar to the federal and state government, tribal administrative law is exceedingly difficult to find. Researchers should not count on being able to access administrative regulations for most tribes without contacting the tribe directly, and many tribes that have administrative courts do not publish those opinions at all. When administrative regulations are made available, they are typically pub-

---

26. *See* https://www.tribalcourtsurvey.org/survey/.
27. *See* http://www.tribal-institute.org/lists/tlpi.htm.
28. *See* http://www.narf.org/nill/ilr/index.html.

lished as part of the tribal code. See Part III.B.1 for more information on finding and researching tribal codes.

4. Intergovernmental Agreements

Tribes sometimes enter into intergovernmental agreements with other governmental bodies, such as a state or county, in order to cooperate on certain matters. For example, in 2013, the Three Affiliated Tribes of the Fort Berthold Reservation entered into an agreement with the state of North Dakota regarding tax and regulation of oil and gas production and extraction.

Unfortunately, there is not one single clearinghouse for tribal intergovernmental agreements. NILL collects some intergovernmental agreements; search its catalog to see what is available. Some tribes also publish intergovernmental agreements with their codes. Finally, some state agencies publish intergovernmental agreements on their websites. For example, the 2013 agreement mentioned in the previous paragraph can be found on the website for the North Dakota Tax Department.[29]

---

29. *See* https://www.nd.gov/tax/oilgas/threeatribes/.

Chapter 16

Federal Equivalents

I. Introduction

The preceding chapters in this book delved into North Dakota legal research. The research tools and techniques, however, are transferable to legal research in other jurisdictions. Lawyers in every state will frequently perform federal legal research. This chapter will familiarize you with federal sources. Note that this chapter is not exhaustive; federal legal research is broad and complex enough to warrant its own book. For more in-depth coverage, consult *Federal Legal Research*.[1]

II. Secondary Sources

As with North Dakota legal research, secondary sources are very helpful when you are unfamiliar with the area of federal law that you're researching. Many secondary sources are aimed specifically at federal law. Among the most helpful and persuasive are the treatises *Wright & Miller's Federal Practice and Procedure* and *Moore's Federal Practice*. To find secondary sources on a particular area of law, search your library catalog or an online database.

III. Researching Enacted Law

A. The U.S. Constitution

1. Background and History

The United States Constitution was written in the summer of 1787 during the Constitutional Convention in Philadelphia. The ratification process for

---

1. *Federal Legal Research* is part of the same series as this book and is directed to similar audiences. The citation is Mary Algero et al., *Federal Legal Research* (2d ed., 2015).

the Constitution lasted three years, until 1790 when Rhode Island ratified it. The same year, the Supreme Court held its first session, under Chief Justice John Jay.

The Constitution establishes the framework for the federal government. Specifically, it divides the government into three branches, the executive, legislative, and judicial. Each branch has specific functions that are intended to provide a well functioning government, with no single branch wielding disproportionate power over the other two. This is called the system of *checks and balances*.

The U.S. Constitution divides power between the federal government and state governments. It further protects individual rights under federal and state law. As noted in Chapter 5, Constitutional Law, federal protections provide a floor to the protection of individual rights, not a ceiling. Many states are more protective of individual rights than the federal constitution requires.

The U.S. Constitution has seven articles: Article I (Legislative Department), Article II (Executive Power), Article III (Judicial Power), Article IV (Relations between States), Article V (Amendment of the Constitution), Article VI (Miscellaneous Provisions), and Article VII (Ratification). It has twenty-seven amendments. The first ten amendments were added in 1791, and they comprise the Bill of Rights. Since 1791, the Constitution has been amended only seventeen times.

2. Locating the Text of the Constitution

The text of the U.S. Constitution is easy to find from both free and commercial sources. It is printed in federal statutory codes, the *United States Code* (U.S.C.), the *United States Code Annotated* (U.S.C.A.), and the *United States Code Service* (USCS). You can find it online on government websites, including the Government Publishing Office website[2] and the U.S. Senate website.[3] Lexis and Westlaw also both provide the text of the U.S. Constitution.

B. Statutes

When Congress enacts new statutes, they are first published as *slip laws*. The slip laws are then compiled into volumes in the order of passage. These compilations are called *session laws* and they are compiled in the *United States Statutes at Large* (commonly referred to as *Statutes at Large*). *Statutes at Large*

---

2. The link is http://www.gpo.gov/fdsys/pkg/CDOC-110hdoc50/pdf/CDOC-110hdoc50.pdf.
3. The link is http://www.senate.gov/civics/constitution_item/constitution.htm.

are organized by congressional session. It is impossible to search the session laws by topic, which makes them fairly difficult to use for research. As a result, the session laws are organized into a *code*. A *code* is a compilation of laws that has been organized by topic. When laws are organized by topic in a code, research becomes much easier.

The *United States Code* is the official codification of United States statutes. The code is organized into 54 topical areas, called *titles*. Each title is then subdivided into chapters, sections, and subsections. The *United States Code* is published every six years; it is updated with annual supplements between publications.

In addition to the *United States Code*, statutes are also published in commercial sources: *United States Code Annotated* (U.S.C.A.), published by West, and *United States Code Service* (U.S.C.S.), published by LexisNexis. These compilations are very effective for research because they are published more quickly than the *United States Code* and they also have publisher's enhancements, like *annotations*. Recall from Chapter 6, Statutes, that *annotations* contain citations to legislative history material, secondary sources, regulations, and cases.

Researching federal statutes is just like researching North Dakota statutes, only in a different jurisdiction. Veteran researchers usually prefer researching statutes in print because they can easily get the context of the entire section and flip back and forth. To research in print, check the index for your search terms and review the results. Be sure to check the pocket part to determine whether there have been any changes to the statute. If you know the name of the statute, you can always check the Popular Name Table in the U.S.C.A. or the U.S.C.S.

You can also find federal statutes online. While veteran researchers tend to prefer researching in print, online sources can be particularly efficient when you know the citation of the statute you're researching. You can find the United States Code on government websites, such as the House of Representatives website.[4]

You can access the U.S.C.A. on Westlaw. To do so, click "Statues & Court Rules." Then, select "United States Code Annotated (USCA)." From there, you can either browse the code, or you can use a search tool listed to the left. The index will usually be the most helpful. When you click on it, you can either browse the index or perform a word search. See Figure 16-1.

You can access the U.S.C.S. on Lexis. To do so, browse sources by publisher. Select "LexisNexis." Then, scroll to find U.S.C.S. From there, you can browse

---

4. The address is http://uscode.house.gov/.

Figure 16-1. Finding Federal Statutes on Westlaw

First, click "Statues & Court Rules."

Then, select "United States Code Annotated (USCA)."

From there, you can either browse the code, or you can use a search tool listed to the left. The index will usually be the most helpful.

Source: Westlaw. Reprinted with permission of Thomson Reuters.

the expandable Table of Contents or you can perform a word search. See Figure 16-2 for a view of the U.S.C.S. Table of Contents.

C. Bill Tracking and Legislative History

The two types of legislation research that researchers need to perform are bill tracking and legislative history. Both are described further below.

1. Bill Tracking

When a *bill*, a piece of pending legislation, may affect a case or a client's interests, you will need to track the bill. The most effective way to track bills is through the Congress.gov website. If you have the bill number, you can

Figure 16-2. U.S.C.S. Table of Contents on Lexis

You can either browse the expandable Table of Contents or perform a word search from the search box at the left of the screen.

Source: Lexis Advance. Reprinted with permission from Reed Elsevier.

simply search by the bill number. Alternatively, if you don't have a bill number, you can search the text of pending bills to either find a specific bill that you know exists, or to see whether there is pending legislation on a particular issue.

2. Legislative History

When you are performing statutory research, the *legislative history* of the statute will sometimes provide background helpful to interpretation of that statute. Legislative history includes past versions of the bill that became the statute, committee hearings, committee reports, and congressional floor debates.

Since the 1970s, lists of the legislative history documents and compilations of the documents themselves have been maintained. Most likely, you will be able to find what you need using the lists and compilations that have already been created.

a. Finding Aids

You can find compiled legislative histories in a variety of places. The easiest place to start is your law library. Many law libraries carry compiled legislative histories for selected laws; if your library does not have what you're looking for, try searching other libraries through OCLC Worldcat union catalog.[5]

Additionally, there are publications that contain lists of legislative history documents for selected laws. *Sources of Compiled Legislative Histories: A Bibliography of Government Documents, Periodical Articles, and Books* lists sources of compiled legislative histories of major federal laws since 1789. You can find this source through HeinOnline. *Union List of Legislative Histories* provides compiled legislative histories for thousands of bills. The list is maintained by the Law Librarians Society of Washington, D.C.

b. Full Compilations

You can find full legislative histories for many laws from a variety of sources. The most comprehensive is the *Congressional Information Service* (C.I.S.), which is available online through ProQuest, an information content provider, via ProQuest Congressional. If you need access to ProQuest Congressional, check with your librarian.

United States Code Congressional and Administrative News (U.S.C.C.A.N.) is more limited than ProQuest Congressional, but it is also more accessible. U.S.C.C.A.N. provides the text of new public laws, the dates when each bill was considered and the volume of the *Congressional Record* that records actions on the floor. U.S.C.C.A.N. also lists the committees that considered the bill, along with cites to committee and conference reports. U.S.C.C.A.N. publishes the most important parts of committee reports. Westlaw offers access to U.S.C.C.A.N.

The Government Accounting Office compiles legislative histories and makes them available to researchers. Like U.S.C.C.A.N., the G.A.O. Legislative History Collection is available on Westlaw.

Lexis also contains legislative histories for some laws. To determine whether Lexis has what you need, browse "Sources" by "Jurisdiction," and check "Statutes and legislation."

In the event that what you need has not been compiled by one of the sources above, you will have to compile the legislative history on your own. Enlist the assistance of a librarian to help you perform this onerous task.

---

5. The address is www.worldcat.org.

D. Administrative Law

Federal regulations are codified in the *Code of Federal Regulations* (C.F.R.). You can search for a relevant regulation in several ways. For example, you could start with a citation that you found through a secondary source or an annotated statute. You can also search the C.F.R. directly. To do this, you could use the print index (although librarians often describe it as unhelpful) or Westlaw's online index. You can browse the table of contents, either in print or online through Lexis, Westlaw, or the Government Publishing Office website.[6] Or you can perform full online text searches.

In addition to using the C.F.R., researchers frequently find the *Federal Register* helpful in administrative law research. The *Federal Register* is a daily publication of agency rules, proposed rules, and public notices. Its chronological organization makes the *Federal Register* an awkward tool for finding regulations. But, it is helpful for providing a historical view of regulations that have been adopted. In this way, the *Federal Register* provides a form of legislative history for regulations. You can access the *Federal Register* on the Government Publishing Office website, as well as on Lexis, Westlaw, and other sites.

E. Court Rules

There are two types of federal court rules: rules of procedure and local rules. Rules of procedure include the Federal Rules of Civil Procedure, the Federal Rules of Criminal Procedure, the Federal Rules of Appellate Procedure, and the Federal Rules of Evidence. Anyone practicing regularly in federal courts should have a print copy of each of these sets of rules and refer to them often. They are published along with federal statutes in the U.S.C., the U.S.C.A., and the U.S.C.S. You can also find them online through both free and commercial sources. For example, court websites provide links to each. Additionally, Cornell University Legal Information Institute (L.I.I.) offers all of the federal rules online for free.[7]

In addition to the procedural rules, courts may also craft rules to govern conduct in particular courts. These are called *local rules*, and they supplement the federal procedural rules. They include items such as deadlines, page limits, and document formatting guidelines. You can access each court's local rules

---

6. The address is www.gpo.gov.
7. The address is www.law.cornell.edu.

online from the court's website; links to all local rules are available on the United States Courts website.[8] Before filing any papers with a federal court, you should always check the local rules.

IV. The Federal Court System and Researching Federal Case Law

A. The Federal Court System

The highest court in the federal system is the United States Supreme Court. The Supreme Court decides cases concerning the U.S. Constitution and federal statutes. Notably, the Supreme Court is not the highest authority on matters of state law (unless, of course, state law potentially violates the U.S. Constitution); the state supreme courts are the highest authority on matters of state law. In almost all circumstances, the Supreme Court has *discretionary jurisdiction*, which means that there is no right to appeal to it. Instead, parties must file a petition for certiorari to ask the Court to hear their case, and the Court then decides whether to hear the case.

The second-highest courts in the federal system are the intermediate courts of appeals, the United States Courts of Appeals. There are thirteen federal judicial circuits. Twelve of the circuits are geographic; included in those twelve are eleven numbered circuits and the D.C. Circuit, which covers the District of Columbia and hears largely administrative cases. North Dakota is in the Eighth Circuit, along with South Dakota, Minnesota, Nebraska, Iowa, Missouri, and Arkansas. The thirteenth circuit, called the Federal Circuit, hears appeals from all circuits concerning patent law and from other specialized courts, like the Court of Federal Claims.[9]

The general jurisdiction trial courts in the federal system are called U.S. District Courts; there are ninety-four districts. Many smaller population states, like North Dakota, have only one federal judicial district. There are, however, federal district courthouses in Bismarck, Fargo, Minot, and Grand Forks. Larger states with heavier caseloads have multiple districts. Missouri, for example, is divided into two districts, eastern and western.

---

8. The address is www.uscourts.gov.
9. For a map of the United States Courts of Appeals, visit www.uscourts.gov.

Table 16-1. Reporters for Federal Court Cases

Court	Reporter	Abbreviation
U.S. Supreme Court	*United States Reports* (official)	U.S.
	Supreme Court Reporter	S. Ct.
	United States Reports, Lawyers' Edition	L. Ed. or L. Ed. 2d
U.S. Court of Appeals	*Federal Reporter*	F. or F.2d or F.3d
U.S. District Courts	*Federal Supplement*	F. Supp. or F. Supp. 2d or F. Supp. 3d

B. Reporters for Federal Cases

Table 16-1 lists the federal reporters and their abbreviations. Each is explained more fully below.

United States Supreme Court decisions are reported in *United States Reports*, the official reporter of Supreme Court decisions. There is frequently lag time between when the Supreme Court decides a case and when *United States Reports* is published. As a result, lawyers frequently cite to one of two unofficial reporters of Supreme Court decisions: *Supreme Court Reporter*, a West publication, and *United States Supreme Court Reports, Lawyers' Edition*, a Lexis publication. You can always access Supreme Court decisions directly from the Court's website.

Cases decided by the United States Courts of Appeals are published in the *Federal Reporter*. There are now three series of the *Federal Reporter*, and cases published there are of the highest precedential value. Cases not selected for publication in the *Federal Reporter* may be published in the *Federal Appendix*, published by West. West began publishing the *Federal Appendix* in 2001. A decision in the *Federal Appendix* may have limited authoritative value because it was not published in the official reporter. This does not mean that you should avoid citing decisions in the *Federal Appendix*. Instead, you should simply be aware of their potential limitations when using them as authority. Again, you can always access Court of Appeals decisions directly from each circuit's website.

Cases decided by the United States District Courts are published in the *Federal Supplement*, now in its third series. You can also access some unpublished district court decisions on Lexis and Westlaw. Remember that these unpublished decisions may be of limited authoritative value.

C. Researching Federal Case Law

As in researching North Dakota case law, digests and text searches will also help you find federal law. You will perform these searches the same way that you would if you were searching for North Dakota cases. The only difference is that your jurisdiction has changed. To the left of the search box at the top, you can access a dropdown menu that will allow you to change your jurisdiction.

About the Authors

Anne E. Mullins is an Assistant Professor at the University of North Dakota School of Law, where she teaches Lawyering Skills, Judicial Writing, and Trial Advocacy. She came to North Dakota after teaching in the University of Oregon School of Law Legal Writing Program. Before entering academia, she practiced complex commercial litigation at Susman Godfrey LLP. She clerked for the Honorable Jacques L. Wiener in the United States Court of Appeals for the Fifth Circuit and the Honorable Sarah S. Vance in the United States District Court for the Eastern District of Louisiana. She earned her J.D. from the University of Chicago Law School and her A.B. from Dartmouth College.

Tammy R. Pettinato is an Assistant Professor and Interim Director of the Law Library at the University of North Dakota School of Law. She teaches Lawyering Skills, Employment Discrimination, and Disability Law. Previously, she taught in the legal writing programs at the University of Louisville School of Law and the University of La Verne College of Law. She also taught Advanced Legal Research at UCLA School of Law. She earned her J.D. from Harvard Law School and her M.S.I. from the University of Michigan.

Index